AAT

AQ2016

Business Tax
(Finance Act 2016)

EXAM KIT

This Exam Kit supports study for the following AAT qualifications:

AAT Professional Diploma in Accounting – Level 4

AAT Level 4 Diploma in Business Skills

AAT Professional Diploma in Accounting at SCQF Level 8

PUBLISHING

British Library Cataloguing-in-Publication Data

A catalogue record for this book is available from the British Library.

Published by:

Kaplan Publishing UK

Unit 2 The Business Centre

Molly Millar's Lane

Wokingham

Berkshire

RG41 2QZ

ISBN: 978-1-78415-637-4

Acknowledgements

We are grateful to HM Revenue and Customs for the provision of tax forms, which are Crown Copyright and are reproduced here with kind permission from the Office of Public Sector Information.

CONTENTS

Features in this exam kit

In addition to providing a wide ranging bank of real assessment style questions, we have also included in this kit:

- unit specific information and advice on assessment technique
- our recommended approach to make your revision for this particular unit as effective as possible.

You will find a wealth of other resources to help you with your studies on the Kaplan and AAT websites:

www.mykaplan.co.uk

www.aat.org.uk/

Quality and accuracy are of the utmost importance to us so if you spot an error in any of our products, please send an email to mykaplanreporting@kaplan.com with full details, or follow the link to the feedback form in MyKaplan.

Our Quality Coordinator will work with our technical team to verify the error and take action to ensure it is corrected in future editions.

INDEX TO QUESTIONS AND ANSWERS

INCOME TAX AND CORPORATION TAX

CHARGEABLE GAINS

NATIONAL INSURANCE CONTRIBUTIONS

CURRENT TAX RELIEFS AND OTHER TAX ISSUES

SELF-ASSESSMENT

ANSWER ENHANCEMENTS

We have added the following enhancements to the answers in this exam kit:

Key answer tips

Some answers include key answer tips to help your understanding of each question.

Tutorial note

Some answers include tutorial notes to explain some of the technical points in more detail.

ASSESSMENT TECHNIQUE

- **Do not skip any of the material** in the syllabus.

- **Read each question** *very* carefully.

- **Double-check your answer** before committing yourself to it.

- Answer **every** question – if you do not know an answer to a multiple choice question or true/false question, you don't lose anything by guessing. Think carefully before you **guess**.

- If you are answering a multiple-choice question, **eliminate first those answers that you know are wrong**. Then choose the most appropriate answer from those that are left.

- **Don't panic** if you realise you've answered a question incorrectly. Getting one question wrong will not mean the difference between passing and failing.

Computer-based assessments – tips

- Do not attempt a CBA until you have **completed all study material** relating to it.

- On the AAT website there is a CBA demonstration. It is **ESSENTIAL** that you attempt this before your real CBA. You will become familiar with how to move around the CBA screens and the way that questions are formatted, increasing your confidence and speed in the actual assessment.

- Be sure you understand how to use the **software** before you start the assessment. If in doubt, ask the assessment centre staff to explain it to you.

- Questions are **displayed on the screen** and answers are entered using keyboard and mouse. At the end of the assessment, you are given a certificate showing the result you have achieved unless some manual marking is required for the assessment.

- In addition to the traditional multiple-choice question type, CBAs will also contain **other types of questions**, such as number entry questions, drag and drop, true/false, pick lists or drop down menus or hybrids of these.

- In some CBAs you may have to type in complete computations or written answers.

- You need to be sure you **know how to answer questions** of this type before you sit the real assessment, through practice.

UNIT SPECIFIC INFORMATION

THE ASSESSMENT

FORMAT OF THE ASSESSMENT

Students will be assessed by computer-based assessment.

In any one assessment, students may not be assessed on all content, or on the full depth or breadth of a piece of content. The content assessed may change over time to ensure validity of assessment, but all assessment criteria will be tested over time.

The learning outcomes for this unit are as follows:

	Learning outcome	Weighting
1	Complete tax returns for sole traders and partnerships and prepare supporting tax computations	29%
2	Complete tax returns for limited companies and prepare supporting tax computations	19%
3	Provide advice on the UK's tax regime and its impact on sole traders, partnerships and limited companies	15%
4	Advise business clients on tax reliefs, and their responsibilities and their agent's responsibilities in reporting taxation to HMRC	19%
5	Prepare tax computations for the sale of capital assets	18%
	Total	100%

Time allowed

2 hours

PASS MARK

The pass mark for all AAT CBAs is 70%.

 Always keep your eye on the clock and make sure you attempt all questions!

DETAILED SYLLABUS

The detailed syllabus and study guide written by the AAT can be found at:

www.aat.org.uk/

REFERENCE MATERIAL

Reference material is provided in this assessment. During your assessment you will be able to access reference material through a series of clickable links on the right of every task. These will produce pop-up windows which can be moved or closed.

ASSESSMENT GUIDANCE

- Some questions ask that answers be calculated to the nearest £. Some answers may require learners to calculate to the nearest £ and pence. If the question does not give any instructions then either method is acceptable and the computer will accept both.

- Some questions have scroll bars at the side. It is important that learners scroll down and do not miss out parts of questions.

- Where free text written answers are required, learners are supplied with a box to type their answers. This scrolls down as far as is necessary to accommodate the learner's answer.

- It is very important to read questions carefully. Common errors which have occurred in the assessments are:

  (i)   Not spotting when amounts are given monthly and not annually

  (ii)   Misreading dates

  (iii) Being unable to work out the number of months in a period when time apportionment is required (e.g. for a partnership 'salary').

- Tasks involving basis period rules or loss relief rules are very badly answered.

- Capital allowance computations – this is a vital area. Tasks involving long or short periods or a cessation are often poorly answered.

KAPLAN'S RECOMMENDED REVISION APPROACH

QUESTION PRACTICE IS THE KEY TO SUCCESS

Success in professional examinations relies upon you acquiring a firm grasp of the required knowledge at the tuition phase. In order to be able to do the questions, knowledge is essential.

However, the difference between success and failure often hinges on your assessment technique on the day and making the most of the revision phase of your studies.

The **Kaplan study text** is the starting point, designed to provide the underpinning knowledge to tackle all questions. However, in the revision phase, poring over text books is not the answer.

Kaplan pocket notes are designed to help you quickly revise a topic area; however you then need to practise questions. There is a need to progress to assessment style questions as soon as possible, and to tie your assessment technique and technical knowledge together.

The importance of question practice cannot be over-emphasised.

The recommended approach below is designed by expert tutors in the field, in conjunction with their knowledge of the chief assessor and the sample assessment.

You need to practise as many questions as possible in the time you have left.

OUR AIM

Our aim is to get you to the stage where you can attempt assessment questions confidently, to time, in a closed book environment, with no supplementary help (i.e. to simulate the real assessment experience).

Practising your assessment technique is also vitally important for you to assess your progress and identify areas of weakness that may need more attention in the final run up to the real assessment.

In order to achieve this we recognise that initially you may feel the need to practise some questions with open book help.

Good assessment technique is vital.

THE KAPLAN REVISION PLAN

Stage 1: Assess areas of strength and weakness

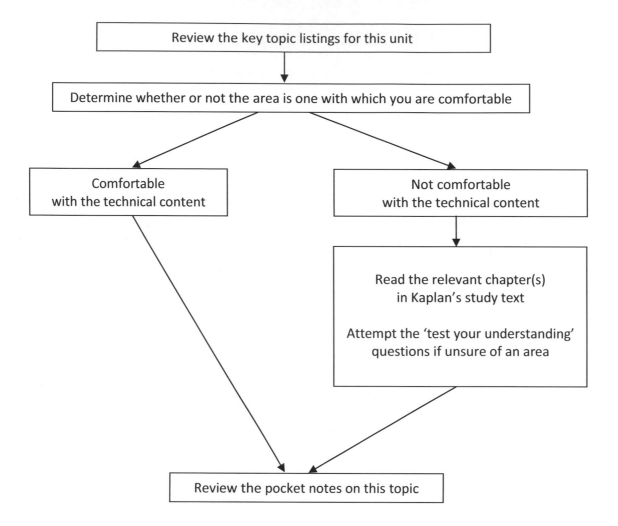

Review the key topic listings for this unit

Determine whether or not the area is one with which you are comfortable

Comfortable
with the technical content

Not comfortable
with the technical content

Read the relevant chapter(s)
in Kaplan's study text

Attempt the 'test your understanding'
questions if unsure of an area

Review the pocket notes on this topic

Stage 2: Practise questions

Follow the order of revision of topics as presented in this kit and attempt the questions in the order suggested.

Try to avoid referring to study texts and your notes and the model answer until you have completed your attempt.

Review your attempt with the model answer and assess how much of the answer you achieved.

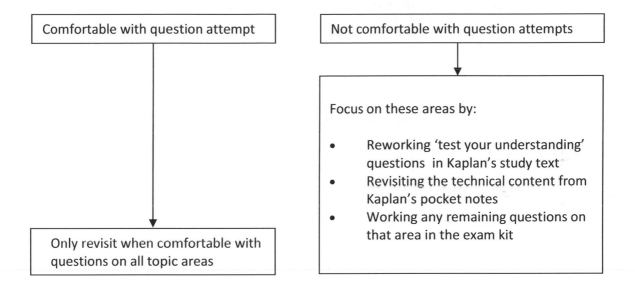

Stage 3: Final pre-real assessment revision

We recommend that you **attempt at least one two hour mock assessment** containing a set of previously unseen real assessment standard questions.

Attempt the mock CBA online in timed, closed book conditions to simulate the real assessment experience.

You will find a mock CBA for this unit at www.mykaplan.co.uk

TAX RATES AND ALLOWANCES

Throughout this exam kit:

1   You should assume that the tax rates and allowances for the tax year 2016/17 and for the Financial Year to 31 March 2017 will continue to apply for the foreseeable future unless you are instructed otherwise.

2   Calculations and workings of tax liability should be made to the nearest penny.

3   All apportionments should be made to the nearest month.

The tax rates and allowances below will be reproduced in the real assessment for business tax.

In addition, other specific information necessary for candidates to answer individual questions will be given as part of the question.

Taxation tables for business tax – 2016/17

Capital allowances

Annual investment allowance

From 1 / 6 April 2014	£500,000
From 1 January 2016	£200,000

Plant and machinery writing down allowance

Long life assets and integral features	8%
Other assets	18%

Motor cars

CO_2 emissions up to 75 g/km	100%
CO_2 emissions between 76 and 130 g/km	18%
CO_2 emissions over 130 g/km	8%

Energy efficient and water saving plant

First year allowance	100%

Capital gains

Annual exempt amount	£11,100
Standard rate (residential property/other disposals)	18/10%
Higher rate (residential property/other disposals)	28/20%
Entrepreneurs' relief rate	10%
Entrepreneurs' relief limit	£10,000,000

National Insurance rates

Class 2 contributions:	£2.80 per week
Small earnings exemption	£5,965 p.a.

Class 4 contributions:

Main rate	9%
Additional rate	2%
Lower earnings limit	£8,060
Upper earnings limit	£43,000

Corporation tax

Financial year	2016	2015
All profits and gains	20%	20%

TAX ADMINISTRATION

This is a useful summary. Much of the following information is given in the Business Tax reference material provided in your assessment but note that items marked with * are not included in the version of the material available at the time of going to print.

Self-assessment – individuals

Election/claim	Time limit	For 2016/17
Pay days for income tax and class 4 NICs	1st instalment: 31 January in the tax year 2nd instalment: 31 July following the end of tax year Balancing payment: 31 January following the end of tax year	31 January 2017 31 July 2017 31 January 2018
Pay day for class 2 NICs*	31 January following the end of the tax year	31 January 2018
Pay day for CGT*	31 January following the end of tax year	31 January 2018
Filing dates If return issued more than 3 months before the filing date	Paper return: 31 October following end of tax year Electronic return: 31 January following end of tax year	31 October 2017 31 January 2018
If return issued less than 3 months before the filing date*	3 months from the date of issue of the return	
Retention of records — Business records	5 years from 31 January following end of the tax year	31 January 2023
— Personal records*	12 months from 31 January following end of the tax year	31 January 2019
HMRC right of repair*	9 months from date the return was filed	
Taxpayer's right to amend a return	12 months from 31 January following end of the tax year	31 January 2019
Repayment relief claim	4 years following end of the tax year	5 April 2021
HMRC can open a compliance check	12 months from submission of the return	
Taxpayer's right of appeal against an assessment*	30 days from the date of the assessment — appeal in writing	

Self-assessment – companies

Election/claim	Time limit
Pay day for companies which are not large	9 months and one day after the end of the chargeable accounting period
Pay day for large companies	Instalments due on 14th day of: – Seventh, Tenth, Thirteenth, and Sixteenth month **after the start** of the chargeable accounting period
Filing dates	Later of: – 12 months from the end of the chargeable accounting period – 3 months from the issue of a notice to deliver a corporation tax return
Companies repayment relief claim*	4 years from the end of the chargeable accounting period
Retention of records	6 years from the end of the chargeable accounting period
HMRC can open a compliance check	12 months from submission of the return
Taxpayer's right of appeal against an assessment*	30 days from the date of the assessment – appeal in writing

PENALTIES

Individuals and companies

Offence		Penalty
Incorrect return	% of revenue lost	
	(tax unpaid as a result of the error)	Maximum %
	Mistake	0
	Failure to take reasonable care	30
	Deliberate understatement	70
	Deliberate understatement with concealment	100
	Penalties can be reduced for taxpayer disclosure	

PENALTIES (CONT)

Offence		Penalty
Late notification*	% of tax unpaid on 31 January following tax year end for individuals and 12 months after the end of the accounting period for companies	
	Percentages as for incorrect returns	
	Penalties can be reduced for taxpayer disclosure	
Failure to keep records	Per tax year or accounting period	£3,000

Individuals

Late payment of tax (cumulative)	% of tax unpaid on 31 January following tax year end	
	More than 30 days late	5% of tax overdue
	More than 6 months late	Further 5% of tax overdue
	More than 12 months late	Further 5% of tax overdue
Late filing (cumulative)	Filed after due date	£100 fixed penalty
	Filed more than three months late	£10 per day for up to 90 days (max £900) in addition to fixed penalty
	Filed more than six months late	5% of tax due plus above penalties (min £300)
	More than 12 months late where withholding information was:	The penalties above plus additional:
	– not deliberate	5% of tax due (min £300)
	– deliberate but no concealment	70% tax due (min £300)
	– deliberate with concealment	100% tax due (min £300)

Companies

Late filing (cumulative)	Less than three months late	£100 fixed penalty
	Filed more than three months late	£200 fixed penalty
	Filed more than six months late	10% of tax due per return
	More than 12 months late	20% of tax due per return

Penalties can be reduced if the taxpayer has a **reasonable excuse**

Section 1

PRACTICE QUESTIONS

INCOME TAX AND CORPORATION TAX

CAPITAL AND REVENUE EXPENDITURE

Key answer tips

Adjustment of profits and determining capital versus revenue expenditure are important areas and likely to be tested. Knowledge of what is treated as capital and what is not is often an area where learners slip up. It is important not to neglect learning facts such as these.

The Business Tax reference material provided in your assessment covers these topics in the sections headed 'Adjustment of profits – sole traders, partnerships and companies' and 'Unincorporated businesses – trading income'.

1   GILES

Giles incurred the following expenditure.

For each item of expenditure, tick the appropriate box to show whether the item is treated as revenue or capital expenditure.

	Revenue	Capital
Decorating an office		
Computer for a salesman		
Office building extension		
Electricity for the quarter to 31 March 2017		
Meal to entertain a customer from Germany		
Fork lift truck for the warehouse		

2 PHILIP

Philip incurred the following expenditure.

For each item of expenditure, tick the appropriate box to show whether the item is treated as revenue or capital expenditure.

	Revenue	Capital
Printer for the office computer		
Water rates		
Legal fees for purchase of a building		

3 BROWN

Brown incurred the following expenditure.

For each item of expenditure, tick the appropriate box to show whether the item is treated as revenue or capital expenditure.

	Revenue	Capital
Repairs to a boiler		
Insurance for motor cars		
Replacement of a severely damaged roof on a newly-purchased warehouse before being able to use the building		
Parking fine incurred by Brown		

4 BADGES OF TRADE

Read the following statements. Tick the appropriate box to show whether or not the individual is likely to be considered to be carrying on a trade.

	Carrying on a trade	Not carrying on a trade
Fred buys a painting in 2009 for £40,000 and hangs it in his home. In 2016 he sells the painting for £50,000 as he needs the cash to pay for a new house.		
Franz regularly buys items in charity shops and then sells them soon after on online auction sites for a higher price. He estimates that each week he has a cash profit of £250 from the sales.		
Each month Jason buys an old car and then repairs it prior to selling it at a profit. He has rented a lock up garage to carry out this work. He uses the money he receives from selling a car to buy the next car.		

ADJUSTMENT OF PROFITS

Key answer tips

Adjustment of profits questions may include a computation starting from the accounting profit where you will need to adjust for disallowed expenses. It is important to carefully read the question and consider each item to decide whether it is allowable or not.

5   JOSEPH FINN

Joseph Finn is self-employed and has a business making widgets.

The business has the following statement of profit or loss for the year ended 31 March 2017:

	£	£
Turnover		1,360,250
Less: Cost of sales		(776,780)
Gross profit		583,470
Wages and salaries	147,280	
Rent and rates	65,280	
Repairs	30,760	
Advertising and entertaining	27,630	
Accountancy and legal costs	16,260	
Motor expenses	38,000	
Leasing costs	8,000	
Telephone and office costs	15,200	
Depreciation	26,525	
Other expenses	101,265	
		(476,200)
Net profit		107,270

Additional information:

1   Repairs include:

	£
Redecorating Joseph's flat	10,000
Decorating business premises	12,000

2   Advertising and entertaining includes:

	£
Gifts to customers:	
Food hampers costing £25 each	1,050
Pens carrying the business's logo, costing £5 each	400
Sponsorship of local charity fete	5,300

3 Motor expenses comprise the running costs of:

	£
Delivery vans	22,000
Sales representative's car	10,000
Joseph's car which is 50% used for private mileage	6,000

4 Leasing costs of £8,000 are for the sales representative's car which has CO_2 emissions of 170 g/km.

5 Other expenses include:

	£
Donation to Children in Need (a national charity)	500
Health and Safety Fine	400

6 Capital allowances have already been calculated at £21,070.

Calculate Joseph Finn's tax adjusted trading profits for the year ended 31 March 2017 using the following pro forma.

Where an item does not require adjustment insert a 0. Where an item is to be deducted from net profit, include it in brackets.

	£	£
Net profit		107,270
Wages and salaries		
Rent and rates		
Repairs		
Advertising and entertaining		
Accountancy and legal costs		
Motor expenses		
Leasing costs		
Telephone and office costs		
Depreciation		
Other expenses		
	———	
		———
Capital allowances		
		———
Adjusted net profit		
		———

6   FLUSH LTD

Flush Ltd incurred the following expenditure.

For each item of expenditure, tick the appropriate box(es) to show whether the item will be treated as allowable or disallowable in the company's adjustment of trading profits computation, and whether or not capital allowances (CAs) will be available.

	Allowable	Disallowable	CAs available
Decorating an office			
Computer for a salesman			
Office building extension			
Electricity for the quarter to 31 March 2017			
Fork lift truck for the warehouse			
Meal to entertain a customer from Italy			
Printer for the office computer			
Interest payable on a loan to purchase an investment property			
Dividends payable			
Costs of a fraud carried out by a director. These costs are not covered by insurance.			

7   JAMIE

Jamie's food manufacturing business has the following statement of profit or loss for the year ended 31 March 2017:

	£	£
Turnover		835,280
Less: Cost of sales		(437,528)
Gross profit		397,752
Wages and salaries	165,948	
Rent, rates and insurance	50,100	
Motor expenses	26,250	
Depreciation	40,355	
Other expenses	137,165	
		(419,818)
Net loss		(22,066)

Additional information:

1   Wages and salaries include:

	£
Jamie	28,000
Jamie's wife Sue, who does not work in the business	12,500
Jamie's daughter, Lisa, the Financial Controller of the business	21,425

2   Motor expenses comprise the running costs of:

	£
Delivery vans	17,940
Salesman's car	6,060
Jamie's motorbike (30% private use)	2,250

3   Other expenses include:

	£
Entertaining customers	625
Entertaining staff (Christmas party)	300
Cost of recipe books given to customers, each with the business logo clearly showing, costing £12.50 each	750
Cost of staff training	1,015

4   Jamie had taken two tins of caviar to eat at home. He paid the business £50 each for these tins. Their selling price was £200 each.

5   Capital allowances have already been calculated at £42,236.

Calculate Jamie's tax adjusted trading profits for the year ended 31 March 2017.

8   CRUSH LTD

Crush Ltd incurred the following expenditure.

For each item of expenditure, tick the appropriate box(es) to show whether the item will be treated as allowable or disallowable in the company's adjustment of trading profits computation, and whether or not capital allowances (CAs) will be available.

	Allowable	Disallowable	CAs available
Water rates			
Building insurance			
Replacement of factory machinery			
Replacement of a severely damaged roof on an office building			
Insurance for motor cars			
Parking fine incurred by an employee			

9   REBECCA

Rebecca runs a beauty salon and lives in the small flat above the salon.

Her business has the following statement of profit or loss for the year ended 31 March 2017:

	£	£
Turnover		351,822
Less: Cost of sales		(208,178)
Gross profit		143,644
Profit on sale of equipment		1,280
		144,924
Professional fees	980	
Impaired debts	1,540	
Repairs and maintenance	340	
Depreciation	7,424	
Heating	2,240	
Rent, rates and insurance	12,000	
Motor expenses	7,780	
Wages and salaries	30,936	
Telephone and office costs	742	
Miscellaneous expenses	1,778	
		(65,760)
Net profit		79,164

Additional information:

1   Professional fees comprise:

	£
Accountancy fees	720
Payroll fees	260

2   Impaired debts comprise:

	£
Increase in specific impaired debt provision	800
Increase in general impaired debt provision	268
Trade debts written off	672
Trade debts recovered	(200)

3   Rent, rates and insurance include expenses relating to the flat where Rebecca lives of £3,000.

4   Motor expenses comprise the running costs of:

	£
Van expenses (van used by Rebecca exclusively for the business)	5,090
Car expenses (car used by Rebecca exclusively for private purposes)	2,690

5   Wages and salaries include Rebecca's drawings of £18,000.

6   Miscellaneous expenses include:

	£
Gifts of diaries to customers costing £7 each and bearing the logo of the business	798
Parking fines incurred by Rebecca in the van	280

7   One of your colleagues has calculated Rebecca's capital allowances to be £11,642.

Calculate Rebecca's tax adjusted trading profits for the year ended 31 March 2017.

10 ARMADILLO

Armadillo is self-employed and his business has made a profit of £34,890 in the year ended 31 March 2017.

This is after the inclusion of the following expenditure:

- Depreciation of £2,345.

- Motor expenses of £4,788. This relates equally to two cars both of which are used 50% for private journeys, one by Armadillo and one by an employee.

- Staff Christmas party of £2,570, which worked out at £257 per head.

- Gift aid donation of £34.

- Wages to Armadillo's wife of £19,000. Other members of staff with the same job in the business are paid £14,500.

- Capital allowances have been calculated at £3,460.

Calculate Armadillo's tax adjusted trading profits for the year ended 31 March 2017.

11 BENABI

Benabi's business has the following statement of profit or loss for the year ended 31 March 2017:

	£	£
Turnover		424,800
Less: Cost of sales		(280,900)
Gross profit		143,900
Wages and salaries	67,400	
Rent, rates and insurance	8,100	
Repairs to plant	3,456	
Advertising and entertaining	6,098	
Accountancy and legal costs	2,400	
Motor expenses	5,555	
Depreciation	8,001	
Telephone and office costs	3,699	
Other expenses	5,702	
		(110,411)
Net profit		33,489

Additional information:

1 Wages and salaries include:

	£
Benabi	6,000
Benabi's wife, who works in the marketing department	8,000

2　　Advertising and entertaining includes:

	£
Gifts to customers:	
Boxes of chocolates, costing £5 each	1,250
Calendars carrying the business's logo, costing £10 each	400
Staff Christmas party for 8 employees	480

3　　Motor expenses include:

	£
Sales manager's car	820
Benabi's car which is only used for private mileage	1,100

4　　Other expenses include:

	£
Cost of staff training	490
Subscription to a local gym for Benabi	220

5　　Capital allowances have already been calculated at £9,955.

Calculate Benabi's tax adjusted trading profits for the year ended 31 March 2017 using the following pro forma.

Where an item does not require adjustment insert a 0. Where an item is to be deducted from net profit, include it in brackets.

	£	£
Net profit		33,489
Wages and salaries		
Rent, rates and insurance		
Repairs to plant		
Advertising and entertaining		
Accountancy and legal costs		
Motor expenses		
Depreciation		
Telephone and office costs		
Other expenses		
	———	
		———
Capital allowances		
		———
Adjusted net profit		
		———

12 FRANKLIN LTD

Franklin Ltd commenced to trade on 1 April 2016 and incurred the following expenditure in its first year of trading to 31 March 2017.

For each item of expenditure, tick the appropriate box to show whether the item will be treated as allowable or disallowable in the adjustment of trading profits computation.

	Allowable	Disallowable
Donation of £500 to Oxfam (a national charity)		
Donation of £100 to the local animal hospital		
Advertising costs incurred in January 2016		
Entertaining prospective customers in February 2016		
Dividends paid to shareholders on 2 January 2017		

CAPITAL ALLOWANCES

Key answer tips

There is likely to be a task in the assessment that will test capital allowances. This may include a capital allowances computation to complete. There is a detailed pro forma computation included in the Business tax reference material provided in your assessment in the section headed 'Capital allowances on plant and machinery'. Note that this pro forma has separate columns dealing with additions qualifying for AIA and for FYA. The answers in this Exam kit use one column which is useful to save space. Either approach is acceptable.

You must also learn the detailed rules regarding the treatment of different types of asset, especially cars, as you may be assessed on the theory behind the capital allowance rules in a separate part of the task.

You must also be able to deal with short or long accounting periods and the period leading up to the cessation of the business.

13 BROAD LTD

Broad Ltd has the following non-current asset information for the year ended 31 December 2016:

	£
Balances brought forward as at 1 January 2016:	
General pool	140,000
Special rate pool	26,000
Additions in May and June 2016:	
Machinery	220,000
Energy saving plant	22,000
Finance Director's car (Citroen)	12,000
Sales Director's car (BMW)	32,000
Plant	10,000

Disposals in June 2016:

Machinery (Cost £10,000)	10,200
Sales Director's car (Vauxhall) (cost £21,000)	13,800

The CO_2 emissions of the cars are:

Citroen   70 g/km

BMW   125 g/km

Vauxhall   180 g/km

All the cars are used 75% for business and 25% privately.

Calculate Broad Ltd's total capital allowances and show the balances to carry forward to the next accounting period.

Use the grid provided for your answer. You have been given more space than you need.

14   WELL LTD

Well Ltd has provided the following information for the year ended 31 December 2016:

	£
Balances brought forward as at 1 January 2016:	
General pool	134,500
Special rate pool	36,000
Additions in February 2016:	
Machinery	244,167
Finance Director's car (Peugeot) (CO_2 emissions 122 g/km)	34,500
Disposals in June 2016:	
Machinery (Cost £12,000)	10,000
Finance Director's car (Toyota) (Cost £13,200)	
(CO_2 emissions 185 g/km)	11,800

Both cars are used 40% privately.

Calculate Well Ltd's total capital allowances and show the balances to carry forward to the next accounting period.

Use the grid provided for your answer. You have been given more space than you need.

15   PINKER LTD

(a)   Pinker Ltd changed its accounting date and has sent you the following information about its non-current assets for the five months accounting period ended 31 December 2016.

Balances brought forward as at 1 August 2016:

General pool   £345,980
Special rate pool   £23,000

In August 2016 the company bought plant for £139,000, a car with CO_2 emissions of 123 g/km for £18,000, and energy saving equipment for £13,790.

Calculate Pinker Ltd's total capital allowances and show the balances to carry forward to the next accounting period.

Use the grid provided for your answer. You have been given more space than you need.

(b)   Which of the following statements about short life assets are true and which are false?

	True	False
Short life assets have a maximum life of 6 years		
Annual investment allowance should be allocated against additions in the special rate and general pool before it is allocated against a short life asset		
Short life assets purchased by X Ltd have a writing down allowance of 18% p.a.		
It is beneficial to claim the short life asset treatment for cars		
Short life asset treatment is compulsory for qualifying assets		

16   SARAH

Sarah's sole trader business has the following non-current asset information for the year ended 31 December 2016:

	£
Balances brought forward as at 1 January 2016:	

	£
General pool	65,100
Sarah's Peugeot car (20% private usage)	14,500
Short life asset (bought in 2012)	7,420

Additions:

	£
Office furniture	11,000
Van	8,600
Sarah's Toyota car – to be used solely for business purposes	20,000
Plant	15,500

Disposals:

	£
Office furniture – original cost higher than disposal value	14,200
Sarah's Peugeot car	10,000
Short life asset	1,400

The CO_2 emissions of the vehicles are:

Peugeot	195 g/km
Van	150 g/km
Toyota	65 g/km

Calculate Sarah's total capital allowances and show the balances to carry forward to the next accounting period.

Use the grid provided for your answer. You have been given more space than you need.

17   DAVE AND NICK

(a)   Dave and Nick formed a partnership and started trading on 1 May 2016.

The partnership made the following non-current asset additions in the period ended 31 December 2016:

	£
Plant	7,680
Office furniture	12,450
Car for Dave, 30% private use, CO_2 emissions 175 g/km	15,300
Car for Nick, 40% private use, CO_2 emissions 120 g/km	10,200

Calculate the partnership's total capital allowances and show the balances to carry forward to the next accounting period.

Use the grid provided for your answer. You have been given more space than you need.

(b)   The partnership does not do well and ceases to trade on 31 December 2017. Further plant had been bought in March 2017 costing £10,000.

When the trade ceased all the plant and furniture was sold for £22,000. Dave and Nick took over their cars at market value of £12,500 and £7,500 respectively.

Calculate the partnership's total capital allowances for the final period of trading.

Use the grid provided for your answer. You have been given more space than you need.

18   PIRBRIGHT LTD

Pirbright Ltd has the following non-current asset information for the year ended 31 December 2016:

		£
Balances brought forward as at 1 January 2016:		
	General pool	81,000
	Special rate pool	28,900
Additions:		
1 May 2016	Machinery	201,900
11 August 2016	Energy saving plant	21,000
1 October 2016	Managing Director's Jaguar car	38,600

				Proceeds £
Disposals:			
26 June 2016	Machinery	Cost £22,000	11,250
1 October 2016	Managing Director's Lexus car	Cost £30,000	15,400

The CO_2 emissions of the vehicles are:

Jaguar   162 g/km

Lexus   175 g/km

The Managing Director used both cars 30% privately.

Calculate Pirbright Ltd's total capital allowances and show the balances to carry forward to the next accounting period.

Use the grid provided for your answer. You have been given more space than you need.

BASIS OF ASSESSMENT

Key answer tips

Basis of assessment for new, ongoing and ceasing businesses as well as partnerships (see the next section) is an important topic. The effect of a change in accounting date can also be tested. Tasks may be broken into a number of smaller tasks rather than one large one.

These rules are covered in the Business tax reference material provided in your assessment in the sections headed 'Sole traders – basis periods', 'Sole traders – change of accounting date' and 'Partnerships'.

It is important to use an appropriate amount of time in the assessment for these tasks, and not to rush your answer.

19 KURT

Kurt started trading on 1 October 2013. He prepares his accounts to 30 June each year.

His tax adjusted trading profits were calculated as follows:

	£
Period to 30 June 2014	22,500
Year to 30 June 2015	43,200
Year to 30 June 2016	47,000

(a) The tax year in which he started trading was:

   A   2012/13

   B   2014/15

   C   2013/14

   D   2015/16

(b) His taxable profits in his first tax year of trading were:

   A   £15,000

   B   £15,750

   C   £22,500

   D   £17,500

(c) His taxable profits in his second tax year of trading were:

   A   £43,200

   B   £39,900

   C   £33,300

   D   £22,500

(d) His taxable profits in his third tax year of trading were:

   A   £47,000

   B   £43,200

   C   £44,150

   D   £46,050

(e)   His overlap profits were:

        [   ]

(f)   Unless Kurt changes his accounting date, his overlap profits are deducted from:

        A   his profits in the second tax year of trading

        B   the profits in the final tax year of trading

        C   the profits in the first tax year of trading

        D   any profits chosen by Kurt

20   ROBERT

Robert started trading on 1 January 2015. He prepares his accounts to 31 October each year.

His tax adjusted trading profits were calculated as follows:

	£
10 months to 31 October 2015	32,000
Year ended 31 October 2016	45,000
Year ended 31 October 2017	87,000

(a)   His taxable profits for 2014/15 were:

        A   £32,000

        B   £9,600

        C   £39,500

        D   £45,000

(b)   His taxable profits for 2015/16 were:

        A   £32,000

        B   £45,000

        C   £39,500

        D   £41,150

(c)   His taxable profits for 2016/17 will be:

        A   £32,000

        B   £45,000

        C   £87,000

        D   £67,750

(d)   His overlap profits were:

        [   ]

21 JAVID

Javid starts trading on 1 January 2016 and draws up his first set of accounts to 31 May 2017.

The period for which his profits will be assessed for the second tax year will be:

A   1 January 2016 to 5 April 2016

B   1 January 2016 to 31 December 2016

C   6 April 2016 to 5 April 2017

D   12 months to 31 May 2017

22 CHARIS

Charis commenced business as a sole trader on 1 January 2016 and prepared her first set of accounts for the period ended 28 February 2017.

In the 14-month period ended 28 February 2017 her tax adjusted trading profit was £21,000.

Her second set of accounts will be for the year ended 28 February 2018 when the tax adjusted trading profits are expected to be £24,000.

What is Charis's trading income assessment for the tax year 2016/17?

A   £21,000

B   £18,000

C   £18,500

D   £24,000

23 GORDON

Gordon ceased trading on 30 November 2016.

Until then, he had been preparing his accounts to 30 June each year.

The tax adjusted trading profits in the final periods of trading were as follows:

	£
Year to 30 June 2015	132,000
Year to 30 June 2016	120,000
Period to 30 November 2016	56,000

He had overlap profits from commencement of trade of £22,000.

(a)   The tax year in which he ceased trading was:

      A   2014/15

      B   2015/16

      C   2016/17

      D   2017/18

(b) His taxable profits in his penultimate tax year of trading were:

A £132,000

B £120,000

C £56,000

D £123,000

(c) His taxable profits in his final tax year of trading were:

A £176,000

B £154,000

C £34,000

D £56,000

(d) When Gordon prepares his final capital allowances computation for the period to 30 November 2016, which of the following types of allowance may be available?

A Annual investment allowance

B Writing down allowance

C First year allowance

D Balancing allowance

24 HENRIETTA

Henrietta started trading on 1 February 2015. She prepares her first set of accounts to 31 May 2016 and then to 31 May each year.

Her tax adjusted trading profits were calculated as follows:

	£
Period to 31 May 2016	7,860
Year to 31 May 2017	8,820
Year to 31 May 2018	15,000

(a) The tax year in which she started trading was:

A 2016/17

B 2013/14

C 2014/15

D 2015/16

(b) Her taxable profits in her first tax year of trading were:

A £7,860

B £3,930

C £983

D £11,790

(c)   Her taxable profits in her second tax year of trading were:

    A   £5,895

    B   £7,860

    C   £8,820

    D   £6,877

(d)   Her taxable profits in her third tax year of trading were:

    A   £15,000

    B   £5,895

    C   £8,820

    D   £8,333

(e)   Her overlap profits were:

(f)   If Henrietta changes her accounting date to 31 August and prepares accounts to 31 August 2019, which one of the following statements is true?

    A   Further overlap profits will be created.

    B   Some of the existing overlap profits will be used up.

25   MELISSA

Mellissa ceased trading on 30 June 2017.

Until then, she had been preparing her accounts to 30 September each year.

The tax adjusted trading profits in the final periods of trading were as follows:

	£
Year to 30 September 2015	13,000
Year to 30 September 2016	12,000
Period to 30 June 2017	5,000

She had overlap profits from commencement of trade of £2,000.

(a)   The tax year in which Melissa ceased trading was:

    A   2014/15

    B   2015/16

    C   2016/17

    D   2017/18

(b)   Her taxable profits in her penultimate tax year of trading were:

    A   £13,000

    B   £12,000

    C   £15,000

    D   £17,000

(c) Her taxable profits in her final tax year of trading were:

A   £3,000

B   £12,000

C   £13,000

D   £5,000

26   ANTONIA

Antonia, a sole trader, has always prepared her accounts to 31 December. She decides to change her accounting date to 30 September by preparing accounts for the nine-month period to 30 September 2016.

Antonia's tax adjusted profits after capital allowances are as follows:

	£
Year to 31 December 2015	38,000
Period to 30 September 2016	46,000
Year to 30 September 2017	52,000

(a)   The tax year of change was:

A   2017/18

B   2016/17

C   2015/16

D   2014/15

(b)   Antonia's taxable profits for the tax year of change were:

A   £74,500

B   £46,000

C   £52,000

D   £59,000

(c)   What is the latest date that Antonia can give notice of the change of accounting date?

A   31 January 2017

B   30 September 2017

C   31 December 2017

D   31 January 2018

(d)   Which of the following statements about change of accounting date is false?

A   A partnership cannot change its accounting date

B   Accounts drawn up to the new accounting date must not exceed 18 months in length

PARTNERSHIPS

27 SUE, WILL AND TERRI

Sue and Will have been in partnership for many years, preparing their accounts to 30 September each year. Their profit sharing ratio was 3:2 respectively.

On 1 April 2016, Terri joined the partnership and the profit sharing ratio was changed to 2:2:1 for Sue, Will and Terri.

For the year ended 30 September 2016, the tax adjusted trading profit was £84,000.

The division of profit would be calculated as:

	Total £	Sue £	Will £	Terri £
Period to: A	B	C	D	

Options:

B	=	£84,000;	£42,000;	£33,600;	£35,000		
C	=	£50,400;	£42,000;	£21,000;	£16,800;	£25,200;	£14,000
D	–	£33,600;	£42,000;	£21,000;	£16,800;	£25,200;	£28,000

	Total £	Sue £	Will £	Terri £
Period to: E	F	G	H	I

Options

F	=	£84,000;	£42,000;	£50,400;	£49,000		
G	=	£42,000;	£33,600;	£16,800;	£14,000;	£25,200;	£20,160
H	=	£42,000;	£33,600;	£16,800;	£14,000;	£25,200;	£20,160
I	=	£19,600;	£14,000;	£16,800;	£8,400;	£10,080	

Insert the appropriate dates in Boxes A and E in the above table.

Choose one number from each of the options above and insert in the appropriate place in the tables above.

28 JENNY AND HARVEY

Jenny and Harvey are in partnership, and have always shared profits equally.

It was then decided that from 1 April 2016 Jenny would be awarded a salary of £40,000 per annum to recognise the extra work that she had taken on.

For the year ended 31 December 2016, the tax adjusted trading profits were £150,000.

Calculate the 2016/17 assessment for each partner.

Jenny	£
Harvey	£

29 SALLY, BARRY, BILL AND BEA

Sally Mander, Barry Cade, Bill Board and Bea Minor have been in partnership for many years, preparing their accounts to 31 May each year. Their profit sharing ratio was 4:2:2:1 respectively after allowing 5% p.a. interest on capital.

On 1 September 2015, they changed the profit sharing ratio to 4:3:2:2 for Sally, Barry, Bill and Bea respectively and decided to have no more interest on capital.

For the year ended 31 May 2016, the tax adjusted trading profit was £756,000.

The partner's capital balances at the start of the period of account were £80,000, £100,000, £200,000 and £90,000 for Sally, Barry, Bill and Bea respectively.

Show the division of profit for the year ended 31 May 2016.

30 ALVIN, SIMON AND THEODORE

Alvin, Simon and Theodore have been in partnership for many years, preparing their accounts to 31 January each year. Their profit sharing ratio was 5:3:2 respectively.

On 1 August 2016, Theodore retired from the partnership and the profit sharing ratio was changed to 1:1 for Alvin and Simon.

For the year ended 31 January 2017, the tax adjusted trading profit was £52,800.

The division of profit would be calculated as:

		Total £	Alvin £	Simon £	Theodore £
Period to:	A	B	C	D	E

Options:

B	= £52,800;	£30,800;	£26,400;	£22,000		
C	= £26,400;	£13,200;	£15,400;	£11,000;	£15,840;	£10,560
D	= £15,840;	£9,240;	£7,920;	£6,600;	£5,940;	£13,200;	£26,400
E	= £10,560;	£8,360;	£3,080;	£4,400;	£4,620;	£2,640;	£5,280

		Total £	Alvin £	Simon £	Theodore £
Period to:	F	G	H	I	

Options:

G	= £52,800;	£26,400;	£22,000;	£30,800		
H	= £26,400;	£13,200;	£11,000;	£15,400;	£17,600;	£7,920
I	= £26,400;	£13,200;	£11,000;	£15,400;	£7,920;	£5,280

Insert the correct dates in Boxes A and F in the above table.

Choose one number from each of the options above and insert in the appropriate place in the tables above.

31   SIAN AND ELLIE

Sian and Ellie have been in partnership for many years, preparing their accounts to 31 July each year. Their profit sharing ratio was 2:1 respectively.

On 1 May 2016, Owen joined the partnership and the profit sharing ratio was changed to 3:2:1 for Sian, Ellie and Owen respectively.

The tax adjusted trading profit was £36,000 for the year ended 31 July 2016, and £60,000 for the year ended 31 July 2017.

What are Owen's assessable profits for 2016/17 and 2017/18?

TRADING LOSSES

Key answer tips

There is likely to be a task in the assessment covering losses for sole traders, partnerships and companies. It may be computational, theory based or a combination of the two. It is important that you understand the difference between the rules applicable to sole traders compared with companies. It is possible that both could be tested in one task – so you must be clear as to which set of rules you are applying.

The Business tax reference material provided in your assessment covers losses in the sections headed 'Trading losses for sole traders and partnerships' and 'Corporation tax – losses'.

32   NICHOLAS

Nicholas, a junior member of the tax department, asks whether the following statements about losses are true or false.

Tick the appropriate box for each statement.

	True	False
A trading loss made by a company can only be offset against trading profits from the same trade when carrying the loss back		
A capital loss made by a company can be offset against trading profits in the year the loss is made and in future years		
A sole trader cannot restrict the amount of loss offset in the current year to preserve the personal allowance		
A sole trader can carry forward a loss for a maximum of 4 years		

33 JOANNA

Which one of the following statements made by Joanna is correct?

A   A loss made by a sole trader must be relieved against total income in the current tax year.

B   For a loss made by a sole trader to be relieved in the current tax year, it must first have been relieved in the preceding tax year.

C   A loss made by a sole trader can only be relieved against profits of the same trade when carried forward to future years.

D   A loss made by a sole trader can be relieved against total income arising in future years.

34 STILTON LTD

Stilton Ltd has the following results for the two years ended 31 December 2017.

Year ended 31 December	2016	2017
	£	£
Trading profits/(loss)	8,000	(40,000)
Bank interest	1,000	600
Chargeable gain	1,200	Nil
Qualifying charitable donation	150	150

Stilton Ltd wishes to use its trading loss as soon as possible.

(a)   How much loss relief can Stilton Ltd claim against current year profits? £ _____

(b)   How much loss relief can Stilton Ltd claim against prior year profits? £ _____

(c)   How much of the loss will then be available to carry forward to future years? £ _____

(d)   How much of the qualifying charitable donation can be carried forward to future years? £ _____

(e)   In future years, what can the trading losses carried forward be relieved against?

    A   Total profits before deducting qualifying charitable donations

    B   Trading profit from any trade

    C   Trading profit from the same trade

    D   Taxable total profits

(f)   Cheddar Ltd had a loss for the year ended 30 June 2017, but continued to trade.

    What is the earliest accounting period in which the company could offset the loss?

    A   Year ended 30 June 2016

    B   Year ended 30 June 2015

    C   Year ended 30 June 2014

    D   Year ended 30 June 2013

35   KANE

Kane asks whether the following statements are true or false.

Tick the appropriate box for each statement.

	True	False
A sole trader can offset a capital loss against chargeable gains in the current and/or the previous tax year, in any order		
Offset of current year capital losses is restricted to leave net gains equal to the annual exempt amount		
A sole trader can offset a trading loss against total income in the current and/or the previous tax year, in any order		
For a trading loss made by a company to be relieved in the preceding accounting period, it must first have been relieved in the current accounting period		
Use of trading loss relief by a company can result in wasted qualifying charitable donations		

36   GREEN LTD

Green Ltd has the following results for the year ended 31 March 2017:

	£
Trading profits	175,000
Interest income	30,000
Net chargeable gains	20,000
Qualifying charitable donation	10,000

The company had trading losses brought forward of £180,000 and capital losses brought forward of £30,000.

(a)   Green Ltd's taxable total profits for the year ended 31 March 2017 are:

A   £5,000

B   £10,000

C   £15,000

D   £20,000

(b)   The trading loss left to carry forward at 31 March 2017 is: £ ____

(c)   The capital loss left to carry forward at 31 March 2017 is: £ ____

(d)   The amount of unrelieved qualifying charitable donation is: £ ____

CORPORATION TAX COMPUTATION

Key answer tips

There is likely to be a task in the assessment that will cover taxable total profits and corporation tax payable. It may be broken into a number of smaller parts and the questions in this section give practice on the individual parts that may be tested in this task.

The Business tax reference material provided in your assessment covers corporation tax in the sections headed 'An outline of corporation tax' and 'The calculation of total profits and corporation tax payable'.

Questions on corporation tax payment dates are included in the payment dates section of this exam kit.

37   WITHERS LTD

The Managing Director of Withers Ltd would like to know the basis upon which items are included in a company's corporation tax computation.

Tick the appropriate box for each item to indicate the basis of assessment for corporation tax purposes.

	Accruals basis	Paid/Receipts basis
Qualifying charitable donations		
Trading income		
Rental income		
Interest income		

38   MORGAN LTD

Morgan Ltd draws up a 15 month set of accounts to 31 March 2017.

What corporation tax computations will need to be prepared?

A   One computation for the whole 15 months.

B   Two computations: one for the 12 months to 31 December 2016 and the other for the 3 months to 31 March 2017.

C   Two computations: one for the 3 months to 31 March 2016 and the other for the 12 months to 31 March 2017.

D   Two computations: the company can choose the lengths as long as neither is more than 12 months.

39 LONG PERIOD OF ACCOUNT

When a company has a long period of account that exceeds 12 months, there are rules on how the income and payments should be apportioned between the chargeable accounting periods.

Tick the appropriate box for each item to indicate how it will be treated for corporation tax purposes.

	Time apportion	Separate computation	Period in which it arises
Chargeable gains			
Capital allowances			
Trading profits			
Qualifying charitable donations			

40 BROUSSE

Brousse asks whether the following statements are true or false.

Tick the appropriate box for each statement.

	True	False
An individual sole trader with a fifteen month period ended 31 March 2017 will have a maximum AIA of £250,000 for capital allowance purposes		
Where a car is provided to a director of a company, the director's private use of the car is not relevant when calculating capital allowances		
An individual sole trader preparing a seventeen month period of account must calculate two separate capital allowances computations; one for the first 12 months and the second for the balancing period		
A company with a nine month accounting period ending on 31 March 2017 will qualify for a 75% (100% × 9/12) first year allowance in respect of the acquisition of a new low emission car		
An individual sole trader with an eleven month accounting period must time apportion the available FYAs by 11/12 for capital allowance purposes		
The maximum AIA for a sole trader business with an eight month accounting period ending 31 December 2016 is £133,333		

41 TAXABLE TOTAL PROFITS

Which ONE of the following statements is correct in relation to the calculation of TTP?

A   Qualifying charitable donations are deductible on an accruals basis

B   Dividend income should be included in TTP

C   Chargeable gains should be excluded from TTP

D   Brought-forward losses are not deductible from TTP

42 COUPE LTD

Coupe Ltd's accounting period is the 15 months ended 31 December 2016.

Its income and payments for the 15 month period are as follows:

	Total	12 months to 30 Sept 2016	3 months to 31 Dec 2016
	£	£	£
Trading income for 15 months ended 31 December 2016	15,750		
Capital allowances (£5,000 for the period ended 30 September 2016, £2,000 for the period ended 31 December 2016)	7,000		
Rental income	7,500		
Interest income (£200 per month, received annually on 31 December)	3,000		
Chargeable gain on asset sold on 1 January 2016	800		
Donation to a national charity paid on 31 December 2016	1,000		

Allocate the total amounts to each of the chargeable accounting periods in the table above.

If no amount is allocated to a box then insert Nil.

43   MERCURY LTD

Mercury Ltd has the following results for the nine months ended 31 March 2017:

	£
Trading profits	250,000
Dividend income	27,000
Chargeable gains	13,000
Qualifying charitable donation	2,000

Mercury Ltd has trading losses brought forward of £35,000 and capital losses brought forward of £22,000.

Calculate Mercury Ltd's corporation tax payable.

44   PANGOLIN LTD

Pangolin Ltd has the following results for the 16 months ended 31 March 2017:

	£
Tax adjusted trading profits	80,000
Rental income	22,000
Chargeable gain on 11 November 2015	61,000
Capital loss on 15 December 2016	53,000
Qualifying charitable donation on 1 July 2016	3,000

The company is not entitled to any capital allowances during this period.

Calculate the total corporation tax liability of Pangolin Ltd for this 16 month trading period.

CHARGEABLE GAINS

Key answer tips

Tasks may cover gains in relation to both individuals and companies and may include questions on chattels, part disposals, chargeable persons, chargeable disposals and connected persons. The task is likely to include a number of smaller questions and may cover a number of different topics, therefore it is important to learn all aspects and ensure you understand them.

It is important to read the questions carefully to ensure that you understand what is being asked and which aspects of chargeable gains are being tested.

The Business tax reference material provided in your assessment covers chargeable gains rules in the sections headed 'Introduction to chargeable gains', 'Calculation of gains and losses for individuals' and 'Calculation of gains and losses for companies'.

EXEMPT ASSETS

45 DEBREL

Debrel disposed of four assets in 2016/17.

Tick the appropriate box to indicate which disposals are chargeable to capital gains tax and which are exempt assets.

	Chargeable asset	Exempt asset
Dishwasher – sold for £300		
Diamond bracelet – sold for £4,000 (cost £2,500)		
Jaguar car – sold for £70,000		
Exchequer stock – sold for £100,000		

46 BIRCH

Birch disposed of three assets in 2016/17.

Tick the appropriate box to indicate which disposals are chargeable to capital gains tax and which are exempt assets.

	Chargeable asset	Exempt asset
Antique vase – sold for £23,000		
Vintage classic car		
Unquoted shares		

47 ROSE

Rose disposed of three assets in 2016/17.

Tick the appropriate box to indicate which disposals are chargeable to capital gains tax and which are exempt assets.

	Chargeable asset	Exempt asset
Holiday cottage		
Quoted shares in an ISA		
Racehorse		

48 LARCH

Larch disposed of three assets in 2016/17.

Tick the appropriate box to indicate which disposals are chargeable to capital gains tax and which are exempt assets.

	Chargeable asset	Exempt asset
Freehold factory		
Diamond necklace – sold for £17,000		
Racing pigeon		

49 ARKWRIGHT

Arkwright disposed of three assets in 2016/17.

Tick the appropriate box to indicate which disposals are chargeable to capital gains tax and which are exempt assets.

	Chargeable asset	Exempt asset
Quoted shares		
Prize winning greyhound		
Painting by Monet – sold for £300,000		

CHARGEABLE GAIN COMPUTATIONS

50 CHARGEABLE GAIN COMPUTATIONS

For each of the following items affecting the calculation of chargeable gains, tick the appropriate box.

	Applies to companies only	Applies to individuals only	Applies to both companies and individuals
(a) Annual exempt amount			
(b) Indexation allowance			
(c) Rollover relief			
(d) Entrepreneurs' relief			

51 WENDY

Wendy asks whether the following statements are true or false.

Tick the appropriate box for each statement.

	True	False
Indexation allowance cannot create an allowable capital loss for companies		
Indexation allowance can create an allowable capital loss for individuals		
The indexation factor is calculated to two decimal places		
The indexation factor is calculated using the movement in the retail prices index from the month of acquisition to the month of disposal		
Indexation allowance is calculated for bonus issues in the share pool of a company		

52 SYLVESTER LTD

Sylvester Ltd sold an antique vase in September 2016 for £5,000.

The vase was bought for £10,000 in September 2006.

The indexation factor from September 2006 to September 2016 was 0.317.

Complete the following computation:

	£
Sale proceeds	
Cost	
Indexation allowance	
Allowable loss	

53 REST LTD

Rest Ltd sold an antique book for £8,000 in December 2016.

It was purchased in December 2008 for £3,000.

The relevant indexation factor is 0.243.

Which of the following is the correct chargeable gain?

A   £Nil – it is an exempt asset

B   £3,333

C   £4,271

D   £5,000

54   XYZ LTD

XYZ Ltd sold a building for £250,000 in January 2017.

The building was purchased for £100,000 in April 2007. An extension was built at a cost of £22,000 in May 2011.

In June 2015 repairs to the roof tiles were made costing £12,000

The indexation factor from April 2007 to January 2017 was 0.291

The indexation factor from May 2011 to January 2017 was 0.127

The indexation factor from June 2015 to January 2017 was 0.024

Complete the following computation:

£

Sale proceeds

Costs

Indexation allowance

Chargeable gain/allowable loss

55   LIVINGSTONE LTD

Livingstone Ltd owns 50 acres of land, which it bought in April 1999 for £180,000.

In November 2016, Livingstone Ltd sold 15 acres for £200,000, when the remaining 35 acres had a market value of £700,000.

The indexation factor from April 1999 to November 2016 was 0.600.

Complete the following computation:

£

Sale proceeds

Cost

Indexation allowance

Chargeable gain

56 STAN

Stan asks whether the following statements are true or false.

Tick the appropriate box for each statement.

	True	False
An individual disposing of one third of his investment land must compare one third of the original cost of the land to the sale proceeds received to calculate the chargeable gain		
A company is 100% owned by Mr Black. The company gifts a capital asset to Mr Black's wife. The gift will be a nil gain/nil loss disposal for capital gains purposes		
Stan is connected to his mother, brother, sister-in-law and niece for the purposes of capital gains tax		
Meera owns a painting which cost £12,000 in 2000. She gives it to a charity in 2016 when the painting is worth £50,000. She has a chargeable gain of £38,000		
Fred bought shares in July 2010 costing £17,500. If Fred dies in 2017 when the shares are worth £40,000, his estate will be charged capital gains tax on a gain of £22,500		

57 TOPHAM LTD

Topham Ltd sold a piece of land for £42,000 in November 2016.

The land was bought for £40,000 in September 2012.

The indexation factor from September 2012 to November 2016 was 0.082.

Complete the following computation:

	£
Sale proceeds	
Cost	
Indexation allowance	
Chargeable gain/allowable loss	

58 SYBILE

Sybile sold two acres of land for £160,000 in October 2016.

Sybile purchased a 45 acre plot of land in June 1991 for £560,000. The market value of her remaining 43 acres in October 2016 was £840,000.

The indexation factor from June 1991 to October 2016 was 0.968.

Complete the following computation:

	£
Sale proceeds	
Cost	
Indexation allowance	
Chargeable gain/allowable loss	

59 RIZWAN

Rizwan asks whether the following statements are true or false.

Tick the appropriate box for each statement.

	True	False
On the disposal of a non-wasting chattel with gross sale proceeds in excess of £6,000 and cost of less than £6,000, the chargeable gain is calculated using deemed sale proceeds of £6,000		
Wasting chattels are exempt if disposed of by individuals or companies		
On the disposal of a non-wasting chattel with gross sale proceeds in excess of £6,000 and cost of less than £6,000, the chargeable gain cannot exceed: 5/3 × (gross sale proceeds − £6,000)		
On the disposal of a non-wasting chattel at a loss with gross sale proceeds and cost in excess of £6,000, the allowable loss is calculated using deemed sale proceeds of £6,000		

60 KAREN, BEN AND SARAH

(a) Karen sold 3 chargeable assets in the year.

She made chargeable gains of £5,000 on Asset 1 and £7,000 on Asset 2. She made a capital loss of £4,000 on Asset 3.

What was her net chargeable gain before deducting the annual exempt amount?

Choose from one of the following options:

£Nil; £8,000; £12,000; £11,100; £900

(b) Ben sold 2 chargeable assets in the year, making gains of £9,000 and £3,600 respectively. He had a capital loss brought forward of £4,000.

What was his net chargeable gain before deducting the annual exempt amount?

Choose from one of the following options:

£Nil; £8,600; £12,600; £11,100; £1,500

(c) In 2016/17 Sarah made a gain of £23,000 in respect of a residential property and £7,000 in respect of a plot of land. She also made a capital loss of £2,000.

She has taxable income of £10,000.

What is her capital gains tax liability for the year?

Choose from one of the following options:

£Nil;   £8,600;   £12,600;   £11,100;   £1,500

DISPOSAL OF SHARES

Key answer tips

There is likely to be a task that will cover disposals of shares. If so, this task is humanly marked and will include a share pool for either an individual or a company, which may include a combination of purchases, disposals, bonus issues and rights issues. The question is likely to be complex with a number of different transactions.

Be careful to remember the matching rules – not all disposals will necessarily be matched with the share pool, therefore it is important to consider these rules first.

The Business tax reference material provided in your assessment covers the rules for disposals of shares in the sections headed 'Shares and securities – disposals by individuals' and 'Shares and securities – disposals by companies'. The material includes the matching rules and a pro forma for the share pool for company disposals.

61 PUCK LTD

Puck Ltd bought 3,000 shares in Quinn Ltd in June 2006 for £12,000.

In January 2010, there was a 1 for 3 bonus issue and in December 2013 there was a 1 for 4 rights issue at £2 a share.

All shares were sold in April 2016 for £24,000.

Indexation factors were:

	January 2010	December 2013	April 2016
June 2006	0.098	0.277	
January 2010		0.163	
December 2013			0.032

Calculate the chargeable gain on the disposal of these shares using the grid supplied.

62   PISTON LTD

Piston Ltd sold all of its ordinary shares in Power plc for £18,800 on 12 May 2016.

Piston Ltd acquired its shares in Power plc as follows:

10 August 2004	Purchased 2,700 shares for £10,640
19 July 2011	Took up a 1 for 3 bonus issue
20 January 2012	Purchased 2,300 shares for £7,130

Indexation factors were:

August 2004 – July 2011	0.252
August 2004 – January 2012	0.270
July 2011 – January 2012	0.014
January 2012 – May 2016	0.100

Calculate the chargeable gain on the disposal of these shares using the grid supplied.

63   DREAM LTD

Dream Ltd bought 6,000 shares in Boat Ltd for £12,000 in March 1998.

In June 2003 there was a bonus issue of 1 for 2.

In December 2016, 7,000 shares were sold for £43,000.

Indexation factors were:

	June 2003	December 2016
March 1998	0.127	0.646
June 2003		0.460

Calculate the chargeable gain on the disposal of these shares using the grid supplied.

64   BATMAN LTD

Batman Ltd bought 7,000 shares in Robin Ltd for £14,000 in May 2004.

It obtained additional shares through a 1 for 8 bonus issue in July 2006 and a 1 for 5 rights issue in July 2010. The rights issue shares were purchased for £3 each.

In September 2016, Batman Ltd sold 5,000 of the shares for £5 per share.

Indexation factors were:

May 2004 to July 2006	0.064
July 2006 to July 2010	0.126
May 2004 to July 2010	0.199
July 2010 to September 2016	0.178

Calculate the chargeable gain on the disposal of these shares using the grid supplied.

65   SHELBYVILLE LTD

On 14 May 2015, Shelbyville Ltd bought 10,000 shares in Springfield plc for £23,300.

On 10 November 2015, Springfield plc issued bonus shares of 1 for 40.

On 29 January 2017, Shelbyville Ltd bought a further 2,000 shares in Springfield plc for £5,950.

On 2 February 2017, Shelbyville Ltd sold 5,875 of these shares for £3.20 each.

Indexation factors were:

May 2015 to November 2015	0.005
November 2015 to January 2017	0.020
November 2015 to February 2017	0.022
May 2015 to January 2017	0.026
May 2015 to February 2017	0.027
January 2017 to February 2017	0.002

Calculate the chargeable gain on the disposal of these shares using the grids supplied.

66   JAMES

James bought 1,000 shares in Sian Ltd for £4,500 in July 2007.

A bonus issue of 1 for 10 shares was made in August 2009.

In October 2016, James sold half the shares for £14.20 per share.

Indexation factors were:

	August 2009	October 2016
July 2007	0.040	0.280
August 2009		0.231

Calculate the chargeable gain on the disposal of these shares.

67 GOODWIN

Goodwin bought 3,600 shares in Shred Ltd for £25,200 on 11 March 2010.

There was a bonus issue of 1 for 3 shares on 23 July 2011.

Goodwin sold 2,500 shares in Shred Ltd for £9.00 per share on 19 January 2017.

On 4 February 2017 Goodwin purchased a further 800 shares in Shred Ltd for £6,800.

Calculate the chargeable gain on the disposal of the shares on 19 January 2017.

CAPITAL GAINS – RELIEFS

Key answer tips

This section covers a broad range of topics, namely capital gains exemptions, reliefs, losses and the calculation of capital gains tax payable.

Reliefs covered are entrepreneurs' relief, gift relief and rollover relief – the latter of which is the only relief available to a company. You should also grasp capital losses and be able to calculate the capital gains tax payable by individuals.

The Business tax reference material provided in your assessment covers these topics in the sections headed 'Introduction to chargeable gains', 'Calculation of gains and losses for individuals', 'Chargeable gains – reliefs available to individuals' and 'Calculation of gains and losses for companies'.

68 SUSAN AND RACHEL

(a) Which of the following statements is correct?

A   Rollover relief is available to individuals and companies

B   Rollover relief is only available to individuals

C   Rollover relief is only available for a qualifying re-investment within 12 months after disposal

D   Rollover relief is only available to companies

(b) Susan, aged 60, made a chargeable gain of £550,000 on the sale of her business. She had owned the business for ten years and is now retiring. She is a higher rate taxpayer.

She also realised a gain of £12,000 on the sale of an antique table.

Which of the following statements is not correct?

A   The chargeable gain on the antique table will be taxed at 20%

B   Entrepreneurs' relief is available on the business gain as all of the conditions have been satisfied

C   The chargeable gain on the business, after the deduction of the annual exempt amount, will be taxed at 10%

D   The annual exempt amount is deducted from the gain on the antique table, leaving all of the business gain to be taxed

(c) Which of the following statements is correct?

A   Individuals can offset their capital losses against their trading profits in the same tax year

B   Individuals can offset their capital losses against their chargeable gains in the same tax year

C   Individuals can offset their capital losses against their total income in the same tax year

D   Individuals get no relief for their capital losses

(d)   Rachel sells an asset to her brother Artie for £15,000 when its market value is £22,000.

Which of the following statements is correct?

A   Artie's deemed cost is £7,000

B   Rachel's deemed gain is £7,000

C   Rachel's deemed proceeds are £15,000

D   Rachel's deemed proceeds are £22,000

69   MALCOLM AND JEREMY

(a)   Malcolm bought a warehouse for £350,000 in March 2008.

In June 2016, it was sold for £725,000.

In the same month he bought a factory for £590,000.

What is the amount of the gain that can be rolled over?

Choose from one of the following options:

£240,000;   £Nil;   £590,000;   £375,000;   £135,000

(b)   Jeremy sold a qualifying business asset on 1 September 2016.

The dates during which the proceeds must be reinvested in another qualifying business asset to be eligible for rollover relief are between:

A	and	B

Choose one date from each of the options below and insert in the appropriate place in the table above.

Options:

A   1 September 2016; 1 September 2013; 6 April 2016; 6 April 2017; 1 September 2015

B   5 April 2017; 5 April 2018; 5 April 2019; 1 September 2015; 1 September 2018; 1 September 2019

70   AVAILABILITY OF RELIEFS

Which one of the following statements is false?

A   Entrepreneurs' relief is only available to individuals

B   Rollover relief is available to both individuals and companies

C   Gift relief is available to both individuals and companies

71   OLIVER LTD

A factory was sold by Oliver Ltd for £800,000 in May 2016 realising a gain of £300,000.

Which of the following statements is correct in relation to rollover relief?

A   If the company reinvests in a qualifying asset within the qualifying time period then the gain of £300,000 is automatically deferred

B   If the company purchases some shares in an unquoted trading company for £880,000 in November 2016 then it can claim rollover relief

C   If the company purchases a replacement factory for £750,000 in June 2017 then it can use rollover relief to defer £250,000 of the gain

D   If the company purchases a replacement factory for £950,000 in June 2019 then it can use rollover relief to defer the gain

72   JOHN, PAUL, GEORGE AND RINGO

(a)   John sells some unquoted trading company shares in June 2016. He does not work for the company.

The shares are sold for their full market value. Three months later, John reinvests all the proceeds in some more unquoted trading company shares.

Which of the following reliefs are available, if any?

A   Rollover relief

B   Entrepreneurs' relief

C   Gift relief

D   None of the above

(b)   Paul gives an antique vase to his son for his birthday. It has a market value of £7,000.

Which of the following reliefs are available, if any?

A   Rollover relief

B   Entrepreneurs' relief

C   Gift relief

D   None of the above

(c)   George sells his 1% interest in unquoted trading company shares to his friend Stuart for £3,000 when their market value is £5,000. The shares cost George £1,000.

Which of the following reliefs are available, if any?

A   Rollover relief

B   Entrepreneurs' relief

C   Gift relief

D   None of the above

(d)   Ringo sells his stake in a partnership business at its full market value. He had been a partner for 3 years before the disposal. He does not reinvest any of the sale proceeds.

Which of the following reliefs are available, if any?

A   Rollover relief

B   Entrepreneurs' relief

C   Gift relief

D   None of the above

73   NORMAN

(a)   Norman has owned 15% of the shares in a trading company since May 1999. He is an employee of the company.

He sells all his shares in December 2016, making a gain before reliefs of £700,000. He has made no other disposals and is a higher rate taxpayer.

What is the capital gains tax payable for 2016/17?

Choose from one of the following options:

£Nil;   £68,890;   £137,780;   £70,000;   £140,000

(b)   What is the deadline for claiming entrepreneurs' relief for a disposal in 2016/17?

Choose from one of the following options:

31 January 2017;   31 January 2018;   31 January 2019;   31 January 2020;
31 October 2017;   31 October 2018;   31 October 2019;   31 October 2020

74   HARRY AND BRIONY

(a)   Which of the following statements is correct?

A   Shares in an individual's personal trading company are qualifying assets for rollover relief.

B   If only part of the proceeds are reinvested in another qualifying asset, the amount that cannot be rolled over is the higher of the proceeds not reinvested and the indexed gain.

C   When rollover relief is claimed, the gain is rolled over by adding it to the base cost of the replacement asset.

D   If a qualifying asset is purchased on 1 October 2016 and another is sold on 25 September 2017, the disposal will qualify for rollover relief.

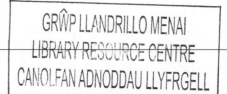

(b)   Harry made a gain qualifying for entrepreneurs' relief of £4,900,000 in 2015/16.

A further qualifying gain of £5,500,000 was made in 2016/17.

There were no other disposals in either year and Harry is a higher rate taxpayer.

What is the capital gains tax payable on the gain in 2016/17?

A   £587,780

B   £550,000

C   £590,000

D   £548,890

(c)   Which of the following statements is correct?

A   Gift relief is only available to companies

B   Gift relief is available to both companies and individuals

C   Gift relief is only available to individuals

(d)   Briony gives an antique vase to her husband, Chris.

Which one of the following statements is correct?

A   Briony's deemed proceeds will be the market value of the vase

B   Briony can claim gift relief for the chargeable gain

C   Briony's chargeable gain will be £Nil

D   Briony's deemed proceeds will be nil so she will have a capital loss

75   CHERYL

(a)   Which one of the following statements is correct?

A   A capital loss made by an individual can be carried back against chargeable gains made in the preceding tax year.

B   A capital loss made by an individual can be carried forward to the following tax year without offsetting it against the current year gains.

C   A capital loss made by an individual which is brought forward from an earlier year is offset against gains in the tax year but only to the extent that it reduces those gains to the amount of the annual exempt amount.

D   A capital loss made by an individual can only be carried forward for one tax year.

(b)   Cheryl gifts an asset to her husband, James.

The asset originally cost Cheryl £50,000.

James immediately sells the asset for its market value of £120,000.

Which one of the following statements is correct?

A   James has a chargeable gain of Nil

B   Both Cheryl and James's unused annual exempt amounts can be used against the gain

C   James's deemed cost is £50,000

D   Cheryl will pay capital gains tax on the gain of £70,000

(c)   Which one of the following statements is correct?

A   Entrepreneurs' relief is available on qualifying business gains of up to £10,000,000 for the lifetime of the taxpayer.

B   Entrepreneurs' relief is restricted to £10,000,000 of gains for each disposal of qualifying business assets.

C   Entrepreneurs' relief is available for individuals and companies.

D   Entrepreneurs' relief is available on the sale of individual business assets.

76   ALLYN AND SIMON

(a)   Allyn bought a factory for £1,400,000 in January 2011.

In November 2016, it was sold for £2,850,000.

In the same month another factory was bought for £2,000,000.

What is the amount of the gain that can be rolled over?

Choose from one of the following options:

£850,000;   £1,450,000;   £600,000;   £1,400,000;   £150,000;   £Nil

(b)   Simon sold a qualifying business asset on 1 February 2015.

The dates during which the proceeds must be reinvested in another qualifying business asset to be eligible for rollover relief are between:

A		B
	and	

Choose one date from each of the options below and insert in the appropriate place in the table above.

Options:

A   1 February 2014; 1 July 2014; 1 February 2012; 6 April 2014; 5 April 2015

B   1 February 2015; 5 April 2015; 1 February 2016; 6 October 2016; 1 February 2017; 1 February 2018

77   EVAN, ZAK AND LILIA

Three taxpayers sold holiday homes during 2016/17 and each has made a chargeable gain of £120,000. They have not made any other disposals during the tax year. The table below shows their taxable income in 2016/17.

Complete the amount of gain that would be chargeable under each of the two rates of capital gains tax. You must enter '0' if your answer is zero.

Taxpayer	Taxable income	Chargeable gain	
		18% CGT	28% CGT
	£	£	£
Evan	21,500		
Zak	29,700		
Lilia	42,300		

78   OPHELIA, GEORGIA AND SID

Three taxpayers sold pieces of land and each has made a taxable gain of £12,000 after deduction of the annual exempt amount. They have not made any other disposals during the tax year. The table below shows their taxable income in 2016/17.

Complete the amount of gain that would be chargeable under each of the two rates of capital gains tax. You must enter '0' if your answer is zero.

Taxpayer	Taxable income	Chargeable gain	
		10% CGT	20% CGT
	£	£	£
Ophelia	35,000		
Georgia	21,200		
Sid	16,850		

NATIONAL INSURANCE CONTRIBUTIONS

SELF-EMPLOYED INDIVIDUALS

Key answer tips

Only classes 2 and 4 are assessable; however, you may be asked to calculate the NICs payable by sole traders or partners.

The Business tax reference material provided in your assessment covers this topic in the section headed 'National insurance contributions'.

79   JENNY AND JACK

(a)   Jenny has self-employed income of £85,000 for 2016/17.

The amount of class 4 NICs payable tax is: £ _____

(b)   Jack has self-employed income of £25,000 for 2016/17.

The amount of class 2 NICs payable tax is: £ _____

(c)   Which of the following statements is correct?

A   Self-employed taxpayers pay class 4 NICs based on the drawings taken out of the business

B   Self-employed taxpayers pay NICs based on the salary they pay to themselves

C   Self-employed taxpayers can pay both class 2 and class 4 NICs

D   Self-employed taxpayers only pay NICs for their employees and not for themselves

80   CARTER

Carter, who has been trading for many years, draws up accounts to 31 December each year.

The results of the business are as follows:

	Accounting profit £	Taxable profit £
Year ended 31 Dec 2016	8,500	6,000
Year ended 31 Dec 2017	7,678	2,500

Which of the following statements is correct?

A   Carter is liable to both class 2 and class 4 for 2016/17

B   Carter is liable to neither class 2 nor class 4 for 2016/17

C   Carter is liable to class 2, but not class 4 for 2016/17

D   Carter is liable to class 4, but not class 2 for 2016/17

81   IVOR

(a)   Ivor's share of his partnership's taxable trading income is £100,000 for 2016/17.

The amount chargeable to class 4 NICs at 9% is: £

(b)   The amount chargeable to class 4 NICs at 2% is: £

(c)   The amount of class 2 NICs payable is: £

(d)   Tick the appropriate box.

	True	False
Ivor will also be required to pay class 1 primary NICs in relation to his salary from the partnership		

82   JAKE, SUE AND PETE

(a)   Jake's sole trader business has made a taxable trading profit of £60,000 for 2016/17.

The amount of class 2 NICs payable by Jake for the year is: £

(b)   Sue has taxable trading profits of £41,000 for 2016/17.

The amount of total class 4 NICs payable by Sue is: £

(c)   Pete's sole trader business has made a taxable trading profit of £4,000 for 2016/17.

The total amount of NICs payable by Pete is: £

83 THOMAS AND SUZANNE

(a) Thomas received a state pension of £6,029 throughout 2016/17 and had self-employed income of £50,000 for 2016/17.

The amount chargeable to class 4 NICs at 9% is: £ |

(b) Suzanne, aged 42, has self-employed income of £35,000 for 2016/17.

The amount of total class 4 NICs payable is: £ |

(c) Which of the following statements is correct?

A   Every self-employed taxpayer must pay class 2 NICs, irrespective of the level of profits

B   Self-employed taxpayers pay both class 2 and class 4, never just one of them

C   Class 4 NICs are based on the accounting profits of the business

D   In a partnership, each partner is responsible for their own NICs

84 AMELIE AND ALEXANDER

Amelie and Alexander are in partnership sharing profits in the ratio 60:40 after paying a salary of £5,000 to Alexander. The partnership's taxable trading profit for the year ended 31 March 2017 was £75,000.

(a) The amount of class 4 NICs payable by Amelie is: £ |

(b) The amount of class 4 NICs payable by Alexander is: £ |

(c) The amount of class 2 NICs payable by Amelie is: £ |

CURRENT TAX RELIEFS AND OTHER TAX ISSUES

R&D TAX CREDITS AND IR35

Key answer tips

This is a new area for Business tax in AQ2016.

The Business tax reference material provided in your assessment covers two topics here - Research and development tax credits and IR35.

85 BARRY

Barry wishes you to tell him which of the following statements are true and which false.

Tick the appropriate box for each statement.

	True	False
Ellis plc is a SME. They have already deducted £40,000 of qualifying research and development cost from their profits. They can deduct a further £92,000 in arriving at their adjusted trading profit.		
Jade plc has annual turnover below 100 million euros. It is automatically classed as an SME.		
The cost of heating and lighting a research and development department can never be part of the qualifying cost for R&D tax credits.		

86 CAITLIN

Caitlin wishes you to tell her which of the following statements are true and which false.

Tick the appropriate box for each statement.

	True	False
Employers' NIC for staff involved in research and development activities can be part of the qualifying cost for R&D tax credits.		
If a SME makes a loss due to qualifying research and development expenditure they must surrender the loss in return for a cash payment.		
Capital expenditure of £50,000 is incurred by a SME on qualifying research and development projects. The company can claim capital allowances on £115,000 (£50,000 × 230%).		

87 JOE

Joe wishes you to tell him which of the following statements are true and which false.

Tick the appropriate box for each statement.

	True	False
All the turnover of a personal service company (PSC) is automatically subject to a deemed employment income tax charge.		
IR35 legislation exists to prevent a PSC from being used to disguise permanent employment.		
If a PSC has only one client it is an indication that this is a disguised employment.		
If a PSC has several clients then none of its income will be subject to an employment income charge.		

88   IRIS

Iris wishes you to tell her which of the following statements are true and which false.

Tick the appropriate box for each statement.

	True	False
Central plc engages Zoom Ltd to provide some consultancy services. Zoom Ltd is a PSC. If the contract between Central plc and Zoom Ltd is deemed to be a relevant engagement under IR35 rules then Central plc must deduct income tax and NIC from the payments made to Zoom Ltd.		
If the owner of a PSC provides their own tools and equipment in carrying out a contract for a client then that contract cannot be deemed to be a relevant engagement subject to IR35 rules.		
If the owner of a PSC cannot send a substitute to carry out work for a client but must perform the work themselves, then that is an indication that the contract may be deemed to be a relevant engagement subject to IR35 rules.		

SELF-ASSESSMENT

Key answer tips

Self-assessment rules and ethics are important areas and can be tested with a written style task or smaller multi-part questions. The task could include questions on the rules relating to payments of tax (including the calculation of payments on account), filing of returns and penalties, as well as the ethics of confidentiality and communication with HMRC.

Payment dates for companies are also covered in this section.

The Business tax reference material provided in your assessment covers these topics in the sections headed 'Payment and administration – sole traders and partners', 'Enquiries and other penalties', 'Corporation tax – payment and administration' and 'Duties and responsibilities of a tax adviser'.

PAYMENT DATES

89 INDIVIDUAL'S PAYMENT DATES

State when the following are due:

(a)   First instalment of income tax for tax year 2016/17:

(b)   Final payment of income tax for tax year 2016/17:

(c)   Capital gains tax payable for tax year 2016/17:

(d)   Second instalment of class 4 NICs for tax year 2016/17:

90 PAYMENTS ON ACCOUNT (POAs)

Tick the appropriate box for each statement.

	True	False
POAs are not required if the income tax payable for the previous year by self-assessment is less than £1,000		
POAs for 2016/17 are due on 31 July 2017 and 31 January 2018		
POAs are not required if more than 80% of the income tax and capital gains tax liability for the previous year was met through tax deducted under PAYE		
POAs of class 2 NICs are never required		
POAs of class 4 NICs are optional; the taxpayer can choose to pay under monthly direct debit or quarterly invoice if they prefer		

91 COMPANY PAYMENT DATES

What is the first payday for corporation tax for a company with augmented profits of £800,000, assuming:

(a)   a 12 month period ended 31 March 2017, a shareholding of 51% in a group company and where the company had similar results in the previous year:

(b)   a nine month period ending 31 December 2016 and no 51% group companies:

(c)   a 12 month period ended 31 January 2017 and no 51% group companies:

(d)   a seven month period ended 31 October 2017, a shareholding of 51% in a group company and was a large company in previous years:

92 DUE DATES

For each of the following statements, fill in the blanks:

(a) An individual pays the second instalment of income tax under self-assessment for 2016/17 on ....

(b) An individual must file their paper income tax return for 2016/17 by ....

(c) A company with augmented profits of £400,000 for the year ended 31 December 2016 must pay its corporation tax by ....

(d) A .... company pays by instalments based on the .... year's profits

93 COMPANY DUE DATES

A company has prepared its accounts for the year ended 31 March 2017.

For the following, state when each are due:

(a) Submission of the corporation tax return:

(b) Payment of corporation tax liability, assuming augmented profits are below £1,500,000:

(c) First instalment of corporation tax liability, assuming the company is required to pay by quarterly instalments:

(d) Final instalment of corporation tax liability, assuming the company is required to pay by quarterly instalments:

ADMINISTRATION, PENALTIES AND ETHICAL STANDARDS

94   IRFAN

Irfan asks whether the following statements are true or false.

Tick the appropriate box for each statement.

	True	False
An individual must retain their tax records for their business for 2016/17 until 5 April 2019		
If an individual is seven months late in submitting their tax return for 2016/17, they will receive a maximum penalty of £200		
The maximum penalty for a mistake in a tax return due to carelessness is 70%		
If an individual's balancing payment for 2016/17 is two months late they can be charged a late payment penalty of 5%		
A company with a period of account ending 30 September 2016 must submit its tax return by 30 September 2017		
Interest is charged on late payments of balancing payments and instalments		

95   COMPLIANCE CHECKS AND APPEALS

(a)   Jane submitted her 2015/16 tax return on 13 January 2017.

By what date must HMRC give notice if they wish to commence a compliance check?

A   31 January 2017

B   31 January 2018

C   13 January 2018

D   30 April 2018

(b)   Jane asks whether the following statements are true or false.

Tick the appropriate box for each statement.

	True	False
A closed compliance check can be reopened within 9 months of the completion notice		
The taxpayer's right of appeal against an amended assessment on the closure of a compliance check must be made within 30 days of the completion notice		
Where a company has submitted its tax return on time, the deadline for HMRC to commence a compliance check is two years after the end of the company's accounting period		

(c) Where the Upper Tier of the Tax Tribunal have determined an appeal on a point of law and the taxpayer expresses dissatisfaction, the case will then be referred to:

A the Court of Appeal and then the Supreme Court (if necessary)

B No one – there is only a right of appeal based on fact

C the European Court of Justice

D the Treasury

96 NAGINA

Nagina asks whether the following statements are true or false.

Tick the appropriate box for each statement.

	True	False
The maximum penalty for failing to keep records is £3,000 per accounting period		
The maximum penalty for a failure to notify chargeability is 100% of the tax due but unpaid		
A late payment penalty can apply to instalment payments of income tax		
Companies can choose whether to file paper tax returns or file online		

97 PENALTIES

(a) What is the maximum penalty for submitting a corporation tax return more than 6 but less than 12 months late?

A £100

B £200 plus 10% of the tax due

C £200

D £200 plus 20% of the tax due

(b) What is the maximum penalty for deliberate understatement without concealment in a tax return?

A £100

B 10% of tax unpaid

C 70% of tax unpaid

D 100% of tax unpaid

(c) What is the penalty for a company's failure to keep records for 6 years?

A Up to £3,000 for each accounting period affected

B Up to £6,000 for each accounting period affected

C Up to £3,000 in total

D Up to £6,000 in total

(d) What is the penalty for late filing of an income tax return if it is less than 3 months late?

A £100

B £200

C £300

D 10% of tax unpaid

98 MANINDER

Maninder asks whether the following statements are true or false.

Tick the appropriate box for each statement.

	True	False
The filing deadline for electronic submission of an individual's 2016/17 tax return is 31 January 2018		
A self-employed individual is required to keep records to support his 2016/17 tax return until 31 January 2023		
There is no penalty for late submission of an individual's tax return as long as it is less than 6 months late		
If a company makes a mistake in the tax return due to failure to take reasonable care, there is a penalty of 30%		
An individual should make their first payment on account for 2016/17 on 31 January 2018		

99 JANET

Janet asks whether the following statements are true or false.

Tick the appropriate box for each statement.

	True	False
If an individual is eight months late in submitting their tax return for 2016/17, they will receive a penalty of £200		
The maximum penalties for errors made by individuals in their tax return vary from 20% to 100%		
If a company fails to keep records for the appropriate period of time, they can be fined up to £2,000		
A company with a period of account ending on 30 June 2016, must keep their records until 30 June 2024		
Late payment penalties are not normally imposed on payments on account		

100 ETHICAL RULES (1)

(a)   Which ONE of the following statements is not correct?

A   Accountants must not associate themselves with returns which contain false or misleading statements

B   Accountants should not be associated with returns which contain information provided recklessly without any real knowledge of whether they are true or false

C   Accountants are allowed to be associated with returns which may omit information which would mislead HMRC

D   Accountants must not be associated with returns which obscure information in a way which would mislead HMRC

(b)   When an accountant is giving a client advice, with whom can he share the information? Choose one option.

A   HMRC

B   Other clients with identical circumstances

C   The client

101 ETHICAL RULES (2)

(a)   Which ONE of the following statements is not correct?

A   Accountants should not be involved with tax returns that omit information

B   Accountants should not be associated with a return that contains misleading information

C   Accountants who are involved with returns that deliberately contain false information can be subject to a penalty

D   Accountants should never prepare tax returns for clients

(b)   When can an accountant divulge confidential information?

A   If the information is over 6 years old

B   If a member of the public asks for it

C   If the accountant has written authority from the client to disclose

D   If the client's spouse requests the information

102 CLIENT ADVICE

(a) Which ONE of the following statements is not correct?

A Accountants need to follow the rules of confidentiality unless given permission by a client

B Accountants can break the rules of confidentiality when the public interest is threatened

C Tax evasion is a legal means of reducing your tax liability

D The AAT expects its members to maintain an objective outlook

(b) When an accountant is advising a client, to whom does he owe the greatest duty of care?

A The accountant's employer

B The AAT

C The client

D The government

103 AAT STUDENT

(a) Which of the following statements is not correct?

A As a student of the AAT you are bound by the duty of confidentiality

B The rules of confidentiality do not need to be followed when a wife asks for information about her husband's tax matters

C The rules of confidentiality need to be followed even after the client relationship has ended

D Confidentiality means not disclosing information you acquire due to your job

(b) When an accountant is working for a client, when can the rules of confidentiality be breached?

A If you do not agree with what the client is saying

B If the client refuses to correct an error in their tax return

C If you resign

D If the client is suspected of money laundering

104 NASHEEN

Nasheen is a student member of the AAT. She asks whether the following statements are true or false.

Tick the appropriate box for each statement.

	True	False
If a husband is ill, it is acceptable to discuss his tax affairs with his wife even if no letter of authorisation exists.		
Accountants must follow the rules of confidentiality irrespective of the situation.		

105 TAX RETURN RESPONSIBILITY

Who is ultimately responsible for ensuring that a taxpayer's tax return is accurately completed?

A   HMRC

B   Tax adviser

C   Taxpayer

D   HM Treasury

106 LAREDO

Laredo asks whether the following statements are true or false.

Tick the appropriate box for each statement.

	True	False
All business tax records for an individual should be kept for at least 4 years.		
The maximum penalty for not keeping records is £2,000.		
An individual whose income tax payable by self-assessment for the previous tax year is less than £1,000 is not required to make payments on account.		
Tax on chargeable gains is paid in two instalments on 31 January in the tax year and 31 July following the end of the tax year.		

WRITTEN QUESTIONS

107 MALIK

Malik has written to you with the following query:

> Further to our earlier conversation, I am writing with a query about national insurance. As you know, in June 2016 I started my own business selling hand-made children's toys and made a taxable profit of £1,200 for the year ended 31 December 2016 and only paid income tax of £850 for the tax year. I paid no national insurance, on your advice. The good news is that I have just been awarded a large contract which will increase my taxable profits significantly for the year ended 31 December 2017. I am still in negotiations at the moment so am not sure of the exact value of the contract, but I hope it will be at least £15,000.
>
> Thanks for explaining the payments on account system for income tax, but can you explain what national insurance contributions I will have to pay as a result of the new contract.
>
> Many thanks

You are required to respond appropriately to Malik's query.

108 BAMBOO LTD

The finance director of Bamboo Ltd has written to your manager with the following query:

> We have a few issues with regard to our tax returns within the group, so can I ask you two questions please?
>
> The financial controller of Ash Ltd has told me that there is an error on the spread sheet that he used to report the rental income for this company for the year ended 30 June 2015 and the rent is understated by £16,000. This is apparently due to a bug in the computer file. He contacted HMRC within a week of discovering the issue and they seem to agree it is a mistake, but what penalty can I expect as a result of this problem?
>
> I have just been told that the corporation tax return for Elm Ltd for the year ended 30 June 2015 was not filed until 7 June 2016, despite my instructions that all returns for all companies in the group should be filed by 1 June 2016. Can you explain any penalties we will incur as a result of this?
>
> Many thanks for your help.

You are required to draft a reply to respond appropriately to this query.

109 SARA

> Your manager has forwarded the following email to you from one of your firm's clients, Sara, who is self-employed.
>
> I received a letter from HMRC yesterday telling me that they are going to commence a compliance check on my 2015/16 income tax return, which I filed 6 months ago. Surely they should have told me earlier? Can you let me know what will happen as a result of this compliance check (should I send them documents?) and what action I can take if I disagree with the findings.

Draft an appropriate response to be passed to your manager.

110 CHARLIE

Charlie has written to you with the following query:

'I am writing to you for some clarification on my tax liabilities. Although I have been paying tax for a long time I still do not understand what needs paying and when.

My tax liability was £8,600 for 2015/16. According to your calculation I will owe £9,000 for 2016/17.

Could you please explain to me how my payments are calculated, and what they should have been for 2016/17 so I can check the HMRC figures.

Many thanks for your time.

Charlie

You need to respond appropriately to his query.

111 MELANIE

Your manager has forwarded the following email to you from Melanie. Melanie is an investment banker and a client of your firm.

'I inherited a number of items of furniture following the death of my father. I renovated the furniture, kept some of the items and sold the rest for a total of £4,000. I know that the items of furniture are exempt for the purposes of capital gains tax, but I am not sure of my position in relation to income tax. Also, I enjoyed the renovation work so much that I am considering purchasing more furniture, which I will then restore and sell at a profit.'

Your manager has provided you with a list of the factors, known as the badges of trade, which will be considered by HM Revenue and Customs in determining whether or not Melanie's activities will be regarded as the carrying on of a trade.

In relation to four of these factors only, explain whether you think Melanie will be treated as carrying on a trade.

112 CHARLOTTE

Charlotte is a new client who has been building up her sole trader business since her retirement in 2012. She has written to you with the following query dated 1 November 2017.

'I wonder if you could explain a few things for me about tax payments. My previous accountants gave me the following information for 2016/17:

	£
Income tax liability	14,580
Less: Tax deducted at source	(5,250)
	9,330
Capital gains tax liability	4,900
	14,230
Tax payable	14,230

I never used to pay any tax by instalments but I paid £4,000 tax on 31 January 2017 and again on 31 July 2017. I don't understand how much I will have to pay on 31 January 2018.

Please can you tell me how much I will have to pay by that date and what happens if I pay my tax late.

I am sure you remember that I don't pay national insurance anymore as I am receiving my state pension.'

You need to respond appropriately to her query.

113 SOPHIA

You have received the following e-mail from Sophia dated 14 September 2017.

> I am a bit worried as I have been receiving interest from a loan to my brother but have never told you about it because I thought it was a private arrangement and not taxable. However my brother says I should have included it on my tax return.
>
> He first started paying me interest in June 2015 so I suppose it should have been included on my 2015/16 tax return. As you are still working on my 2016/17 return it will not be a problem to alter that.
>
> Please advise what we should do now and the consequences of this mistake. The interest was £1,500 in 2015/16 and £1,800 in 2016/17.

You should reply to Sophia's email. Sophia is a higher rate taxpayer.

TAX RETURNS

Key answer tips

The three tax returns which can be tested are sections from the self-employed return, the partnership return and the corporation tax return.

It is vital that you are careful to complete the correct boxes on the return – it is not enough to just enter the right numbers somewhere! Care and attention to detail are crucial to score full marks in this task.

114 HUMMEL LTD

Complete the return below as far as is possible using the following information.

In the year ended 31 December 2016 Hummel Ltd made sales of £1,000,000 leading to a taxable trading profit of £585,000.

The company also had rental profits of £200,000, interest income of £20,000 and chargeable gains of £110,000.

The company had trading losses brought forward of £47,000 and capital losses brought forward of £4,900.

Tax calculation

Turnover

145 Total turnover from trade £ ☐☐☐☐☐☐☐☐☐☐☐☐☐☐ . 0 0

150 Banks, building societies, insurance companies and other financial concerns –
put an 'X' in this box if you do not have a recognised turnover and have not made an entry in box 145 ☐

Income

155 Trading profits £ ☐☐☐☐☐☐☐☐☐☐ . 0 0

160 Trading losses brought forward claimed against profits £ ☐☐☐☐☐☐☐☐☐☐ . 0 0

165 Net trading profits – *box 155 minus box 160* £ ☐☐☐☐☐☐☐☐☐☐ . 0 0

170 Bank, building society or other interest, and profits from non-trading loan relationships £ ☐☐☐☐☐☐☐☐☐☐ . 0 0

172 Put an 'X' in box 172 if the figure in box 170 is net of carrying back a deficit from a later accounting period ☐

175 Annual payments not otherwise charged to Corporation Tax and from which Income Tax has not been deducted £ ☐☐☐☐☐☐☐☐☐☐ . 0 0

180 Non-exempt dividends or distributions from non-UK resident companies £ ☐☐☐☐☐☐☐☐☐☐ . 0 0

185 Income from which Income Tax has been deducted £ ☐☐☐☐☐☐☐☐☐☐ . 0 0

190 Income from a property business £ ☐☐☐☐☐☐☐☐☐☐ . 0 0

195 Non-trading gains on intangible fixed assets £ ☐☐☐☐☐☐☐☐☐☐ . 0 0

200 Tonnage Tax profits £ ☐☐☐☐☐☐☐☐☐☐ . 0 0

205 Income not falling under any other heading £ ☐☐☐☐☐☐☐☐☐☐ . 0 0

Chargeable gains

210 Gross chargeable gains £ ☐☐☐☐☐☐☐☐☐☐ . 0 0

215 Allowable losses including losses brought forward £ ☐☐☐☐☐☐☐☐☐☐ . 0 0

220 Net chargeable gains – *box 210 minus box 215* £ ☐☐☐☐☐☐☐☐☐☐ . 0 0

Profits before deductions and reliefs

225 Losses brought forward against certain investment income £ ☐☐☐☐☐☐☐☐☐☐ . 0 0

230 Non-trade deficits on loan relationships (including interest) and derivative contracts (financial instruments) brought forward £ ☐☐☐☐☐☐☐☐☐☐ . 0 0

235 Profits before other deductions and reliefs – *net sum of boxes 165 to 205 and 220 minus sum of boxes 225 and 230* £ ☐☐☐☐☐☐☐☐☐☐ . 0 0

115 ROYLE LTD

Complete the return below as far as is possible using the following information.

Royle Ltd's corporation tax computation for the year ended 31 October 2016 is as follows:

	£	£
Turnover		2,900,000
Adjusted trading profits		350,000
Property income		20,000
Interest income		6,000
Dividend income		
Chargeable gains for the year	18,000	
Less: Capital loss b/f	(3,800)	
		14,200
Total profits		390,200
Less: Qualifying charitable donation		(15,200)
Taxable total profits		375,000

Tax calculation

Turnover

145	Total turnover from trade	£ ⬚⬚⬚⬚⬚⬚⬚⬚⬚⬚⬚⬚⬚⬚ • 0 0
150	Banks, building societies, insurance companies and other financial concerns – *put an 'X' in this box if you do not have a recognised turnover and have not made an entry in box 145*	⬚

Income

155	Trading profits	£ ⬚⬚⬚⬚⬚⬚⬚⬚⬚⬚⬚ • 0 0
160	Trading losses brought forward claimed against profits	£ ⬚⬚⬚⬚⬚⬚⬚⬚⬚⬚⬚ • 0 0
165	Net trading profits – *box 155 minus box 160*	£ ⬚⬚⬚⬚⬚⬚⬚⬚⬚⬚⬚ • 0 0
170	Bank, building society or other interest, and profits from non-trading loan relationships	£ ⬚⬚⬚⬚⬚⬚⬚⬚⬚⬚⬚ • 0 0
172	Put an 'X' in box 172 if the figure in box 170 is net of carrying back a deficit from a later accounting period	⬚
175	Annual payments not otherwise charged to Corporation Tax and from which Income Tax has not been deducted	£ ⬚⬚⬚⬚⬚⬚⬚⬚⬚⬚⬚ • 0 0

180	Non-exempt dividends or distributions from non–UK resident companies	£ ⬚⬚⬚⬚⬚⬚⬚⬚⬚⬚⬚ • 0 0
185	Income from which Income Tax has been deducted	£ ⬚⬚⬚⬚⬚⬚⬚⬚⬚⬚⬚ • 0 0
190	Income from a property business	£ ⬚⬚⬚⬚⬚⬚⬚⬚⬚⬚⬚ • 0 0
195	Non-trading gains on intangible fixed assets	£ ⬚⬚⬚⬚⬚⬚⬚⬚⬚⬚⬚ • 0 0
200	Tonnage Tax profits	£ ⬚⬚⬚⬚⬚⬚⬚⬚⬚⬚⬚ • 0 0
205	Income not falling under any other heading	£ ⬚⬚⬚⬚⬚⬚⬚⬚⬚⬚⬚ • 0 0

Chargeable gains

210	Gross chargeable gains	£ ⬚⬚⬚⬚⬚⬚⬚⬚⬚⬚⬚ • 0 0
215	Allowable losses including losses brought forward	£ ⬚⬚⬚⬚⬚⬚⬚⬚⬚⬚⬚ • 0 0
220	Net chargeable gains – *box 210 minus box 215*	£ ⬚⬚⬚⬚⬚⬚⬚⬚⬚⬚⬚ • 0 0

Profits before deductions and reliefs

225	Losses brought forward against certain investment income	£ ⬚⬚⬚⬚⬚⬚⬚⬚⬚⬚⬚ • 0 0
230	Non-trade deficits on loan relationships (including interest) and derivative contracts (financial instruments) brought forward	£ ⬚⬚⬚⬚⬚⬚⬚⬚⬚⬚⬚ • 0 0
235	Profits before other deductions and reliefs – *net sum of boxes 165 to 205 and 220 minus sum of boxes 225 and 230*	£ ⬚⬚⬚⬚⬚⬚⬚⬚⬚⬚⬚ • 0 0

116 JORDAN

Complete the return below as far as is possible using the following information.

Boxes 17 to 31 have already been completed.

Included in the expenses listed in Jordan's personal income tax return, the following information is relevant:

1   Irrecoverable debts written off comprise:

	£
Increase in specific irrecoverable debt provision	800
Increase in general irrecoverable debt provision	268
Trade debts written off	672
Trade debts recovered	(200)

2   Rent, rates and insurance include:

	£
Expenses relating to the flat where the owner lives	3,000

3   Motor expenses include:

	£
Van expenses (van used by owner exclusively for the business)	5,090
Car expenses (car used by owner exclusively for private purposes)	2,690

4   Wages and salaries include:

	£
Owner's drawings	18,000

5   Miscellaneous expenses include:

	£
Gifts of diaries to customers	
– costing £8 each and bearing the logo of the business	800
Parking fines incurred by owner	280

Business expenses

Please read the 'Self-employment (full) notes' before filling in this section.

Total expenses	Disallowable expenses
If your annual turnover was below £83,000, you may just put your total expenses in box 31	Use this column if the figures in boxes 17 to 30 include disallowable amounts

17 Cost of goods bought for resale or goods used
£ 208178 · 00

32 £ · 00

18 Construction industry – payments to subcontractors
£ · 00

33 £ · 00

19 Wages, salaries and other staff costs
£ 35604 · 00

34 £ · 00

20 Car, van and travel expenses
£ 13112 · 00

35 £ · 00

21 Rent, rates, power and insurance costs
£ 14240 · 00

36 £ · 00

22 Repairs and renewals of property and equipment
£ 340 · 00

37 £ · 00

23 Phone, fax, stationery and other office costs
£ 742 · 00

38 £ · 00

24 Advertising and business entertainment costs
£ · 00

39 £ · 00

25 Interest on bank and other loans
£ · 00

40 £ · 00

26 Bank, credit card and other financial charges
£ · 00

41 £ · 00

27 Irrecoverable debts written off
£ 1540 · 00

42 £ · 00

28 Accountancy, legal and other professional fees
£ 980 · 00

43 £ · 00

29 Depreciation and loss/profit on sale of assets
£ 6144 · 00

44 £ · 00

30 Other business expenses
£ 1778 · 00

45 £ · 00

31 Total expenses (total of boxes 17 to 30)
£ 282658 · 00

46 Total disallowable expenses (total of boxes 32 to 45)
£ · 00

SA103F 2016   Page SEF 2

117   MR BODDERS

Complete the return below as far as is possible using the following information.

Boxes 17 to 31 have already been completed.

Included in the expenses listed in Mr Bodders' personal income tax return, the following information is relevant:

1   Mr Bodders has taken drawings of £3,000. This is included in salaries expense.

2   Advertising and entertaining includes:

	£
Gifts to customers:	
Bottles of wine costing £10 each	1,500
Electronic diaries carrying the business's logo, costing £70 each	210
Staff Christmas party for 20 employees	2,000
Client entertaining	600

3   Motor expenses include:

	£
Sales manager's car	6,915
Mr Bodders' car (60% private usage)	2,400

4   Rent, rates and power include:

	£
Electricity for Mr Bodders' house (which is not used in the business)	4,000

Business expenses

Please read the 'Self-employment (full) notes' before filling in this section.

Total expenses

If your annual turnover was below £83,000, you may just put your total expenses in box 31

Disallowable expenses

Use this column if the figures in boxes 17 to 30 include disallowable amounts

17 Cost of goods bought for resale or goods used

£ 1 0 8 1 9 5 . 0 0

32 £ . 0 0

18 Construction industry – payments to subcontractors

£ . 0 0

33 £ . 0 0

19 Wages, salaries and other staff costs

£ 6 5 6 5 0 . 0 0

34 £ . 0 0

20 Car, van and travel expenses

£ 1 0 1 1 0 . 0 0

35 £ . 0 0

21 Rent, rates, power and insurance costs

£ 1 2 2 5 0 . 0 0

36 £ . 0 0

22 Repairs and renewals of property and equipment

£ . 0 0

37 £ . 0 0

23 Phone, fax, stationery and other office costs

£ 2 7 5 5 . 0 0

38 £ . 0 0

24 Advertising and business entertainment costs

£ 8 6 6 5 . 0 0

39 £ . 0 0

25 Interest on bank and other loans

£ . 0 0

40 £ . 0 0

26 Bank, credit card and other financial charges

£ . 0 0

41 £ . 0 0

27 Irrecoverable debts written off

£ 5 1 0 . 0 0

42 £ . 0 0

28 Accountancy, legal and other professional fees

£ 2 9 8 0 . 0 0

43 £ . 0 0

29 Depreciation and loss/profit on sale of assets

£ 1 6 1 4 0 . 0 0

44 £ . 0 0

30 Other business expenses

£ 1 7 6 0 . 0 0

45 £ . 0 0

31 Total expenses (total of boxes 17 to 30)

£ 2 2 9 0 1 5 . 0 0

46 Total disallowable expenses (total of boxes 32 to 45)

£ . 0 0

SA103F 2016   Page SEF 2

118 LYNNE AND SHIRLEY PETERS

Complete the return below for the partnership as a whole and for Lynne Peters using the following information.

Lynne and Shirley Peters have traded in partnership for many years as social event organisers, sharing profits 3:2.

Their tax adjusted trading profits for the year ended 31 March 2017 are £230,400, and the partnership received bank interest of £6,210.

The partnership also paid a charge of £4,000 and had £2,800 of CIS deductions made by contractors on account of tax.

PARTNERSHIP STATEMENT (SHORT) for the year ended 5 April 2017

Please read these instructions before completing the Statement

Use these pages to allocate partnership income if the only income for the relevant return period was trading and professional income or taxed interest and alternative finance receipts from banks and building societies. Otherwise you must download or ask the SA Orderline for the 'Partnership Statement (Full)' pages to record details of the allocation of all the partnership income. Go to **www.gov.uk/self-assessment-forms-and-helpsheets**

Step 1 Fill in boxes 1 to 29 and boxes A and B as appropriate. Get the figures you need from the relevant boxes in the Partnership Tax Return. Complete a separate Statement for each accounting period covered by this Partnership Tax Return and for each trade or profession carried on by the partnership.

Step 2 Then allocate the amounts in boxes 11 to 29 attributable to each partner using the allocation columns on this page and page 7, read the Partnership Tax Return Guide, go to www.gov.uk/self-assessment-forms-and-helpsheets If the partnership has more than 3 partners, please photocopy page 7.

Step 3 Each partner will need a copy of their allocation of income to fill in their personal tax return.

PARTNERSHIP INFORMATION
If the partnership business includes a trade or profession, enter here the accounting period for which appropriate items in this statement are returned.

Start **1** / /

End **2** / /

Nature of trade **3**

MIXED PARTNERSHIPS

Tick here if this Statement is drawn up using Corporation Tax rules **4**

Tick here if this Statement is drawn up using tax rules for non-residents **5**

Individual partner details

6 Name of partner

Address

Postcode

Date appointed as a partner (if during 2015–16 or 2016–17) **7** / /

Partner's Unique Taxpayer Reference (UTR) **8**

Date ceased to be a partner (if during 2015–16 or 2016–17) **9** / /

Partner's National Insurance number **10**

Partnership's profits, losses, income, tax credits, etc

Partner's share of profits, losses, income, tax credits, etc

Copy figures in boxes 11 to 29 to boxes in the individual's **Partnership (short)** pages as shown below

Tick this box if the items entered in the box had foreign tax taken off ▼

- **for an accounting period ended in 2016–17**

from box 3.83 Profit from a trade or profession	**A**	**11** £	Profit **11** £	Copy this figure to box 8
from box 3.82 Adjustment on change of basis		**11A** £	**11A** £	Copy this figure to box 10
from box 3.84 Loss from a trade or profession	**B**	**12** £	Loss **12** £	Copy this figure to box 8
from box 10.4 Business Premises Renovation Allowance		**12A** £	**12A** £	Copy this figure to box 15

- **for the period 6 April 2016 to 5 April 2017***

from box 7.9A UK taxed interest and taxed alternative finance receipts	**22** £	**22** £	Copy this figure to box 28
from box 3.97 CIS deductions made by contractors on account of tax	**24** £	**24** £	Copy this figure to box 30
from box 3.98 Other tax taken off trading income	**24A** £	**24A** £	Copy this figure to box 31
from box 7.8A Income Tax taken off	**25** £	**25** £	Copy this figure to box 29
from box 3.117 Partnership charges	**29** £	**29** £	Copy this figure to box 4, 'Other tax reliefs' section on page Ai 2 in your personal tax return

* if you are a 'CT Partnership' see the Partnership Tax Return Guide

SA800 2016 PARTNERSHIP TAX RETURN: PAGE 6

Section 2

ANSWERS TO PRACTICE QUESTIONS

INCOME TAX AND CORPORATION TAX

CAPITAL AND REVENUE EXPENDITURE

1   GILES

	Revenue	Capital
Decorating an office	✓	
Computer for a salesman		✓
Office building extension		✓
Electricity for the quarter to 31 March 2017	✓	
Meal to entertain a customer from Germany	✓	
Fork lift truck for the warehouse		✓

2   PHILIP

	Revenue	Capital
Printer for the office computer		✓
Water rates	✓	
Legal fees for purchase of a building		✓

Tutorial note

Costs relating to the purchase of a capital asset will be included as part of its capital cost. Hence the legal fees incurred on purchase of the building should be debited to capital not revenue expenses. For tax purposes legal fees related to a capital acquisition are always treated as capital expenditure and disallowed in the computation of adjusted profits.

3 BROWN

	Revenue	Capital
Repairs to a boiler	✓	
Insurance for motor cars	✓	
Replacement of a severely damaged roof on a newly-purchased warehouse before being able to use the building		✓
Parking fine incurred by Brown	✓	

Tutorial note

1   *Expenditure to repair a newly acquired asset is normally treated as revenue expenditure if the asset is in a serviceable condition when purchased.*

However, where the asset cannot be used in the business unless further expenditure is incurred on it, and the purchase price reflects the state of disrepair, any subsequent repair expenditure is treated as part of the original capital cost of purchase of the asset.

2   *The parking fine of the owner is a revenue expense and will be deducted in the statement of profit or loss of the business.*

It is not a tax allowable expense; however this question does not require you to consider that aspect.

4 BADGES OF TRADE

	Carrying on a trade	Not carrying on a trade
Fred buys a painting in 2009 for £40,000 and hangs it in his home. In 2016 he sells the painting for £50,000 as he needs the cash to pay for a new house.		✓
Franz regularly buys items in charity shops and then sells them soon after on online auction sites for a higher price. He estimates that each week he has a cash profit of £250 from the sales.	✓	
Each month Jason buys an old car and then repairs it prior to selling it at a profit. He has rented a lock up garage to carry out this work. He uses the money he receives from selling a car to buy the next car.	✓	

Tutorial note

In order to decide if an individual is trading it is often useful to look at the 'Badges of Trade' which are tests originally developed by a Royal Commission in the 1950s.

These include:

Subject matter (S)

Length of ownership (O)

Frequency of transactions (F)

Improvements or supplementary work (I)

Circumstances of realisation (R)

Profit motive (M).

These are listed in the Business tax reference material provided in your assessment in the section headed ' The badges of trade'.

Other factors are also taken Into account by HMRC such us the source of funds to buy items.

Applying these tests to the above situations:

Fred bought a painting to enjoy at home. He has sold only one painting in a 7 year period. This is not frequent. He has been forced to sell to raise cash and he will not be considered to be trading.

Franz has regular transactions, buying items specifically to sell and not for personal enjoyment. He does not keep the items for a long time. He makes a profit and is likely to be considered as trading.

Jason frequently buys and sells cars. He undertakes supplementary work on the cars and has hired premises to carry out the work. He finances the purchase of the cars with the profits from previous cars. He is likely to be considered to be trading.

ADJUSTMENT OF PROFITS

Key answer tips

The chief assessor has commented in the past that when learners have failed in this type of task, it seems to be due to lack of robust knowledge on areas such as lease payments, adjustments for private use by the owner of the business and what is capital and what is not. A common error would be to adjust for the business use element of the expenses as opposed to adjusting for the private element.

5 JOSEPH FINN

Tax adjusted trading profit computation – year ended 31 March 2017

	£	£
Net profit		107,270
Wages and salaries	0	
Rent and rates	0	
Repairs	10,000	
Advertising and entertaining	1,050	
Accountancy and legal costs	0	
Motor expenses (50% × £6,000)	3,000	
Leasing costs (15% × £8,000)	1,200	
Telephone and office costs	0	
Depreciation	26,525	
Other expenses (£500 + £400)	900	
	———	42,675
		———
		149,945
Capital allowances		(21,070)
		———
Adjusted net profit		128,875
		———

Tutorial note

1   *Gifts to customers costing less than £50 per person per year and carrying a conspicuous advertisement for the business are tax allowable. However, gifts of food, drink and tobacco are not allowable.*

2   *15% of the leasing costs for high emission cars (CO_2 emissions over 130 g/km) are disallowed.*

3   *The donation to Children in Need is a donation to a national charity and is not allowable in the adjustment of profits computation. Provided the donation is made under the gift aid rules, tax relief is available for the donation in Joseph's personal income tax computation. The operation of this relief is covered in personal tax.*

6   FLUSH LTD

	Allowable	Disallowable	CAs available
Decorating an office	✓		
Computer for a salesman		✓	✓
Office building extension		✓	
Electricity for the quarter to 31 March 2017	✓		
Fork lift truck for the warehouse		✓	✓
Meal to entertain a customer from Italy		✓	
Printer for the office computer		✓	✓
Interest payable on a loan to purchase an investment property		✓	
Dividends payable		✓	
Costs of a fraud carried out by a director. These costs are not covered by insurance.		✓	

Tutorial note

There are no capital allowances available on office buildings.

Entertaining customers (UK or overseas) is not allowable.

Interest on loans for a non-trading purpose, such as buying an investment, is disallowed in the adjusted profit computation but is allowed as a deduction from non-trading interest received.

Note that despite the loan being in relation to an investment property, for companies the interest is not deducted against property income. All interest payable for non-trading purposes is deducted from interest income.

Dividends payable are not an allowable expense.

The costs of a fraud carried out by directors are not allowable. If the fraud had been carried out by an employee the costs would have been allowed.

7   JAMIE

Tax adjusted trading profit computation – year ended 31 March 2017

	£	£
Net loss		(22,066)
Add: Depreciation	40,355	
Jamie's salary	28,000	
Jamie's wife's salary	12,500	
Jamie's motorbike (30% × £2,250)	675	
Entertaining customers	625	
Caviar (2 × £150)	300	
	———	82,455
		60,389
Less: Capital allowances		(42,236)
Tax adjusted trading profit		18,153

Tutorial note

1   Salaries paid to family members are allowable provided they represent reasonable remuneration for the services provided to the business. As Jamie's wife does not work for the business at all, none of that expense is allowable. It is assumed, however, that the salary paid to his daughter for her role as Financial Controller of the business is reasonable remuneration.

2   Entertaining staff is allowable for the business, irrespective of the amount spent. Any other form of entertaining is not allowable.

3   Gifts to customers costing less than £50 per person per year and carrying a conspicuous advertisement for the business are tax allowable. Therefore the recipe book expenditure will be allowable.

4   Where the owner takes goods out of the business, for tax purposes, it is treated as a sale to himself at full market value. Jamie must therefore account for the profit element of the transaction (£200 – £50 = £150 per tin of caviar) in his adjustment of profit computation.

8   CRUSH LTD

	Allowable	Disallowable	CAs available
Water rates	✓		
Building insurance	✓		
Replacement of factory machinery		✓	✓
Replacement of a severely damaged roof on an office building	✓		
Insurance for motor cars	✓		
Parking fine incurred by an employee	✓		

Tutorial note

1   Replacement of the whole of an asset such as the factory machinery is a capital item. The replacement of part of an asset, such as the damaged roof of the office building will be treated as revenue expenditure.

2   Parking fines incurred by non-senior employees whilst on business activity are allowable for tax purposes.

9   REBECCA

Tax adjusted trading profit computation – year ended 31 March 2017

	£	£
Net profit		79,164
Add: Depreciation	7,424	
Increase in general impaired debt provision	268	
Expenses relating to Rebecca's flat	3,000	
Rebecca's car expenses	2,690	
Rebecca's drawings	18,000	
Parking fines	280	
	———	31,662
		———
		110,826
Less: Profit on sale of equipment	1,280	
Capital allowances	11,642	
	———	(12,922)
		———
Tax adjusted trading profit		97,904
		———

Tutorial note

1   *If a sole trader makes a general provision in the accounts, it is not allowable for tax purposes, but specific provisions are allowable.*

2   *Gifts to customers costing less than £50 per person per year and carrying a conspicuous advertisement for the business are tax allowable. Therefore the cost of the diaries will be allowable.*

3   *Parking fines incurred by the owner are not allowable, even if they are incurred whilst on business activity.*

10   ARMADILLO

Tax adjusted trading profit computation – year ended 31 March 2017

	£	£
Net profit		34,890
Add: Depreciation	2,345	
Motor expenses (£4,788 × 50% × 50%)	1,197	
Gift aid donation	34	
Excess wages to wife (£19,000 – £14,500)	4,500	
	———	8,076
		———
		42,966
Less: Capital allowances		(3,460)
		———
Tax adjusted trading profit		39,506
		———

Tutorial note

1   *50% of the motor expenses relates to Armadillo. Of that 50%, only 50% are allowable as he uses his car 50% for private purposes.*

2   *Entertaining staff is allowable for the business, irrespective of the amount spent.*

3   *The gift aid donation is not allowable in the adjustment of profits computation. Tax relief is available for the donation in Armadillo's personal income tax computation. The operation of this relief is covered in personal tax.*

4   *Salaries paid to family members are allowable provided they represent reasonable remuneration for the services provided to the business. As Armadillo's wife is paid more than the normal salary for the role she performs, the excess is not allowable.*

11   BENABI

Tax adjusted trading profit computation – year ended 31 March 2017

	£	£
Net profit		33,489
Wages and salaries – Benabi's salary	6,000	
Rent, rates and insurance	0	
Repairs to plant	0	
Advertising and entertaining – Boxes of chocolates	1,250	
Accountancy and legal costs	0	
Motor expenses – Benabi's motor expenses	1,100	
Depreciation	8,001	
Telephone and office costs	0	
Other expenses – subscription to gym	220	
	———	16,571
		50,060
Capital allowances		(9,955)
Adjusted net profit		40,105

Tutorial note

1 Salaries paid to family members are allowable provided they represent reasonable remuneration for the services provided to the business. It is assumed that £8,000 is reasonable remuneration for Benabi's wife working in the marketing department.

2 Gifts to customers costing less than £50 per person per year and carrying a conspicuous advertisement for the business are tax allowable. However, gifts of food, drink and tobacco are not allowable.

3 Entertaining staff is allowable for the business, irrespective of the amount spent.

4 Personal expenses, such as the subscription to the gym for the owner, are not allowable.

12 FRANKLIN LTD

	Allowable	Disallowable
Donation of £500 to Oxfam (a national charity)		✓
Donation of £100 to the local animal hospital	✓	
Advertising costs incurred in January 2016	✓	
Entertaining prospective customers in February 2016		✓
Dividends paid to shareholders on 2 January 2017		✓

Tutorial note

Donations to charity are not allowable in the adjustment of trading profits computation, with the exception of small donations to local charities.

Any donation to a national charity is not allowable in the adjustment of trading profits.

If not allowable in the adjustment of trading profits computation, relief is given as an allowable deduction from total profits in the computation of the company's taxable total profits.

Pre-trading expenditure is allowable if it is incurred in the 7 years before trade commences and is expenditure that would be allowable if trade had commenced. The advertising is allowable but the entertaining would not be allowable if trade had started so is not allowable if incurred before trade starts.

Dividends are appropriations of profit and not allowable as an expense.

CAPITAL ALLOWANCES

Key answer tips

In previous assessments, the biggest area of confusion has been the handling of cars. Remember that their treatment depends on the CO_2 emissions and whether they are used privately by the owner of the business – you must know the WDA available in each case and which column they should be included in. Always consider whether private use needs to be adjusted for – remember no adjustment is ever required for private use in a company, nor for the private use of an employee in a sole trader's business.

The final areas of difficulty are long periods of account for a company (which must be split into two separate periods) and the handling of capital allowances when a business ceases trading (remember no AIA, WDA or FYA should be given, simply a balancing adjustment in each column).

13 BROAD LTD

Capital allowances computation – year ended 31 December 2016

	£	General pool £	Special rate pool £	Total £
TWDV b/f		140,000	26,000	
Additions – no AIA				
Sales director's car		32,000		
Additions – with AIA				
Machinery	220,000			
Plant	10,000			
	230,000			
Less: AIA	(200,000)			200,000
		30,000		
Disposals (lower of cost and SP)		(10,000)	(13,800)	
		192,000	12,200	
Less: WDA (18%/8%)		(34,560)	(976)	35,536
Addition – 100% FYA				
Energy saving plant	22,000			
Low emission car	12,000			
	34,000			
Less: FYA (100%)	(34,000)			34,000
		Nil		
TWDV c/f		157,440	11,224	
Total allowances				269,536

Tutorial note

1   *Private use of assets by an employee is irrelevant in a company's capital allowances computation; the allowances are available in full. The individual is assessed on the private use element in their personal income tax computation as an employment benefit.*

2   *Capital allowances on car purchases are calculated based on the CO_2 emissions of the car as follows:*

    –   *new car with CO_2 emissions of ≤ 75 g/km:*

        eligible for a FYA of 100% (i.e. Finance Director's car)

    –   *CO_2 emissions of between 76 – 130 g/km:*

        put in main pool and eligible for a WDA at 18% (i.e. Sales Director's car)

    –   *CO_2 emissions of > 130 g/km:*

        put in special rate pool and eligible for a WDA at 8% (i.e. Sales Director's car sold)

3   *Disposals are deducted at the lower of cost and sale proceeds. The deduction for the machinery is therefore restricted to £10,000.*

14   WELL LTD

Capital allowances computation – year ended 31 December 2016

		General pool	Special rate pool	Total
	£	£	£	£
TWDV b/f		134,500	36,000	
Additions – no AIA or FYA				
Finance Director's car		34,500		
Additions – with AIA				
Machinery	244,167			
Less: AIA	(200,000)			200,000
		44,167		
Disposals (Lower of Cost and SP)		(10,000)	(11,800)	
		203,167	24,200	
Less: WDA				
18%		(36,570)		36,570
8%			(1,936)	1,936
TWDV c/f		166,597	22,264	
Total allowances				238,506

Tutorial note

1   *Private use of assets is irrelevant in a company's capital allowances computation; the allowances are available in full. The individual is assessed on the private use element in their personal income tax computation as an employment benefit.*

2   *Capital allowances on car purchases are calculated based on the CO_2 emissions of the car. As the Finance Director's new car has CO_2 emissions of between 76 – 130 g/km; it is put in the main pool and is eligible for a WDA at 18%.*

The Finance Director's original car had CO_2 emissions of 185 g/km and would therefore have been in the special rate pool.

3   *Disposals are deducted at the lower of cost and sale proceeds.*

15   PINKER LTD

(a)   **Capital allowances computation – five months ended 31 December 2016**

		General pool	Special rate pool	Total
	£	£	£	£
TWDV b/f		345,980	23,000	
Additions – no AIA or FYA				
Car		18,000		
Additions – with AIA				
Plant	139,000			
Less: AIA (£200,000 × 5/12)	(83,333)			83,333
		55,667		
		419,647	23,000	
Less: WDA (18% × 5/12)		(31,474)		31,474
Less: WDA (8% × 5/12)			(767)	767
Addition – 100% FYA				
Energy saving plant	13,790			
Less: FYA (100%)	(13,790)			13,790
		Nil		
TWDV c/f		388,173	22,233	
Total allowances				129,364

Tutorial note

1 *This computation is for the five month period ending 31 December 2016. Therefore you must remember to time apportion the AIA and WDAs available by 5/12, but not the FYA.*

2 *Private use of assets is irrelevant in a company's capital allowances computation. The allowances are available in full. The individual is assessed on the private use element in their personal income tax computation as an employment benefit.*

3 *Capital allowances on car purchases are calculated based on the CO_2 emissions.*

 Cars with CO_2 emissions of between 76 – 130 g/km are put in the main pool and are eligible for a WDA at 18% per annum.

(b) **Short life assets**

	True	False
Short life assets have a maximum life of 6 years		✓
Annual investment allowance should be allocated against additions in the special rate and general pool before it is allocated against a short life asset	✓	
Short life assets purchased by X Ltd have a writing down allowance of 18% p.a.	✓	
It is beneficial to claim the short life asset treatment for cars		✓
Short life asset treatment is compulsory for qualifying assets		✓

Tutorial note

Short life assets can have an unlimited useful life however it may be beneficial to claim short life asset treatment where an asset has an expected life of less than 8 years. A short life asset is de-pooled in the year of purchase and kept in a single asset pool column. If it has not been sold within eight years of the end of the accounting period in which it was purchased its tax written down value is transferred to the general pool at the start of the following year.

The short life asset election is not permitted for cars.

Short life asset treatment must be claimed, it is not compulsory.

16 SARAH

Capital allowances computation – year ended 31 December 2016

	£	General pool £	Peugeot car (B.U. 80%) £	Short life asset £	Total £
TWDV b/f		65,100	14,500	7,420	
Additions – with AIA					
Furniture	11,000				
Van	8,600				
Plant	15,500				
	35,100				
Less: AIA	(35,100)				35,100
		Nil			
Disposals (lower of cost and SP)		(14,200)	(10,000)	(1,400)	
		50,900	4,500	6,020	
Balancing allowance			(4,500) × 80%	(6,020)	9,620
Less: WDA (18%)		(9,162)			9,162
Addition – 100% FYA					
Low emission car	20,000				
Less: FYA (100%)	(20,000)				20,000
		Nil			
TWDV c/f		41,738			
Total allowances					73,882

Tutorial note

1   *Private use of assets by the owner is relevant and allowances must be restricted to the business use proportion only.*

2   *Capital allowances on car purchases are calculated based on the CO_2 emissions.*

     New cars with CO_2 emissions of ≤ 75 g/km are low emission cars and eligible for a FYA of 100%.

3   *CO_2 emissions are irrelevant for vans. Vans are eligible for the AIA and any balance goes into the general pool.*

4   *Short life assets may be de-pooled and when sold a balancing allowance (or charge) will arise.*

17 DAVE AND NICK

(a) **Capital allowances computation – eight months ended 31 December 2016**

		General pool	Dave's car (B.U. 70%)	Nick's car (B.U. 60%)	Total
	£	£	£	£	£
Additions – no AIA or FYA					
Car			15,300	10,200	
Additions – with AIA					
Plant	7,680				
Furniture	12,450				
	20,130				
Less: AIA	(20,130)				20,130
		Nil			
Less: WDA (8% × 8/12)			(816) × 70%		571
Less: WDA (18% × 8/12)				(1,224) × 60%	734
TWDV c/f		Nil	14,484	8,976	
Total allowances					21,435

Tutorial note

1   *The partnership commenced on 1 May 2016 and the first accounts are prepared to 31 December 2016. This computation is therefore for an eight month period. Remember to time apportion the WDAs available by 8/12. The AIA is also time apportioned but the maximum amount of £133,333 (£200,000 × 8/12) exceeds the purchases in the period.*

2   *Capital allowances on car purchases are calculated based on the CO_2 emissions of the car as follows:*

   –   *new car with CO_2 emissions of ≤ 75 g/km:*

       eligible for a FYA of 100% (i.e. none in this question)

   –   *CO_2 emissions of between 76 – 130 g/km:*

       eligible for a WDA at 18% (i.e. Nick's car)

   –   *CO_2 emissions of > 130 g/km:*

       eligible for a WDA at 8% (i.e. Dave's car)

3   *Remember to calculate the allowance in full on the private use cars and then adjust for private use (i.e. only claim the business proportion of the allowance).*

(b)   **Capital allowances computation – period ended 31 December 2017**

	General pool	Dave's car (B.U. 70%)	Nick's car (B.U. 60%)	Total
	£	£	£	£
TWDV b/f	Nil	14,484	8,976	
Plant	10,000			
	10,000			
Disposal	(22,000)			
Disposal – MV		(12,500)	(7,500)	
	(12,000)	1,984	1,476	
Balancing charge	12,000			(12,000)
Balancing allowances		(1,984)	(1,476)	
		× 70%	× 60%	886
Net balancing charge				(11,114)

Tutorial note

When a business ceases to trade there is no AIA or WDA in the final accounting period. Additions are added to the relevant columns. Proceeds are compared to the WDV of each column and balancing charges or allowances calculated.

Remember that only the business proportion of balancing allowances/balancing charges can be claimed/charged.

18 PIRBRIGHT LTD

Capital allowances computation – year ended 31 December 2016

	£	General pool £	Special rate pool £	Total £
TWDV b/f		81,000	28,900	
Additions – car (no AIA or FYA)			38,600	
Additions – with AIA				
Machinery	201,900			
Less: AIA	(200,000)			200,000
		1,900		
Disposals (lower of cost and SP)		(11,250)	(15,400)	
		71,650	52,100	
Less: WDA				
18%		(12,897)		12,897
8%			(4,168)	4,168
Addition – 100% FYA				
Energy saving plant	21,000			
Less: FYA (100%)	(21,000)			21,000
		Nil		
TWDV c/f		58,753	47,932	
Total allowances				238,065

Tutorial note

1   *Private use of assets is irrelevant in a company's capital allowances computation; the allowances are available in full. The individual is assessed on the private use element in their personal income tax computation as an employment benefit.*

2   *Capital allowances on car purchases are calculated based on the CO_2 emissions of the car. A car with CO_2 emissions in excess of 130 g/km is put into the special rate pool and is eligible for a WDA at 8%.*

BASIS OF ASSESSMENT

Key answer tips

When applying the basis of assessment rules be careful to start with the correct tax year, as otherwise this will have a knock on effect on the rest of your answer. You must also carefully count months, as any mistakes with this simple task will cost you marks. It is recommended that you work your answers on paper first – checking the dates and months, and ensuring that the dates seem logical. Remember that a taxpayer will always be taxed on twelve months' worth of profits, except in the first and last tax year of the business.

19   KURT

   (a)   C

   (b)   A

   (c)   C

   (d)   B

   (e)   £25,800

   (f)   B

Working

Tax year	Basis period	Assessment £
2013/14	1 October 2013 – 5 April 2014 (6/9 × £22,500)	15,000
2014/15	1 October 2013 – 30 September 2014 £22,500 + (3/12 × £43,200)	33,300
2015/16	Current year basis year ended 30 June 2015	43,200
Overlap profits	1 October 2013 – 5 April 2014 (6/9 × £22,500)	15,000
	1 July 14 – 30 September 2014 (3/12 × £43,200)	10,800
		25,800

20   ROBERT

   (a)   B

   (b)   C

   (c)   B

   (d)   £17,100

Working

Tax year	Basis period		Assessment £
2014/15	1 January 2015 – 5 April 2015 (3/10 × £32,000)		9,600
2015/16	1 January 2015 – 31 December 2015 £32,000 + (2/12 × £45,000)		39,500
2016/17	Current year basis year ended 31 October 2016		45,000
Overlap profits	1 Jan 2015 – 5 Apr 2015	(3/10 × £32,000)	9,600
	1 Nov 2015 – 31 Dec 2015	(2/12 × £45,000)	7,500
			———
			17,100
			———

21 JAVID

Answer = C

Working

Tax year	Basis period
2015/16	1 January 2016 – 5 April 2016
2016/17	6 April 2016 – 5 April 2017

Tutorial note

The first tax year is the year in which the business commenced trading, i.e. 2015/16, therefore the second tax year is 2016/17. The opening year rules dictate that when a business does not have a year end falling inside of a tax year (2016/17) then the profits will be taxed on an actual basis (i.e. 6 April – 5 April).

22 CHARIS

Answer = B

Working

Tax year	Basis period	Assessment £
2015/16	1 January 2016 – 5 April 2016 (3/14 × £21,000)	4,500
2016/17	1 March 2016 – 28 February 2017 (12/14 × £21,000)	18,000
2017/18	Current year basis year ended 28 February 2018	24,000

Tutorial note

Where the period of account ending in the second tax year is more than 12 months then the basis period is the 12 months to the accounting date ending in the second tax year, i.e. 12 months to 28 February 2017.

23 **GORDON**

(a)   C

(b)   A

(c)   B

(d)   D

Working

Tax year	Basis period	Assessment £
2015/16	Penultimate year of assessment Current year basis year ended 30 June 2015	132,000
2016/17	Final period of assessment 1 July 2015 – 30 November 2016 Year ended 30 June 2016 5 months ended 30 November 2016	120,000 56,000
		176,000
	Less: Overlap profits	(22,000)
		154,000

24 **HENRIETTA**

(a)   C

(b)   C

(c)   A

(d)   B

(e)   £4,913

(f)   B

Working

Tax year	Basis period	Assessment £
2014/15	1 February 2015 – 5 April 2015 (2/16 × £7,860)	983
2015/16	6 April 2015 – 5 April 2016 (12/16 × £7,860)	5,895
2016/17	12 months ended 31 May 2016 (12/16 × £7,860)	5,895
Overlap profits	1 June 2015 – 5 April 2016 (10/16 × £7,860)	4,913

Tutorial note

There is no set of accounts ending in the second tax year, 2015/16, so the assessment is based on the profits in the tax year 6 April 2015 – 5 April 2016.

If Henrietta changes her accounting date to 31 August (I.e. later in the tax year), then the assessment for 2019/20, the year of change, will be based on 15 months of profits. Three months of existing overlap profits will be used to reduce the assessment.

25   MELISSA

(a)   D

(b)   B

(c)   A

Working

Tax year	Basis period	Assessment £
2016/17	Penultimate year of assessment Current year basis year ended 30 September 2016	12,000
2017/18	Final period of assessment 1 October 2016 – 30 June 2017 Less: Overlap profits	5,000 (2,000)
		3,000

26 ANTONIA

(a) B

(b) A

(c) D

(d) A

Working

Tax year	Basis period	Assessment £
2015/16	Year to 31 December 2015	38,000
2016/17	12 months to the new accounting date of 30 September 2016	
	Three months to 31 December 2015 (£38,000 × 9/12)	28,500
	Nine months to 30 September 2016	46,000
		74,500

Tutorial note

Antonia must give notice of the change in the 2016/17 tax return which must be filed by 31 January 2018.

PARTNERSHIPS

Key answer tips

The allocation of assessable profits between partners is another area of difficulty that the chief assessor has highlighted in the past.

27   SUE, WILL AND TERRI

Allocation of profit

	Total £	Sue £	Will £	Terri £
Period to: A = 31 March 2016 (£84,000 × 6/12) Allocate (3:2)	B = 42,000	C = 25,200	D = 16,800	
Period to: E = 30 September 2016 (£84,000 × 6/12) Allocate (2:2:1)	F = 42,000	G = 16,800	H = 16,800	I = 8,400
	84,000	42,000	33,600	8,400

28   JENNY AND HARVEY

Allocation of profit

	Total £	Jenny £	Harvey £
Period to: 31 March 2016 (£150,000 × 3/12)	37,500		
Allocate (1:1)		18,750	18,750
Period to: 31 December 2016 (£150,000 × 9/12) Salary (£40,000 × 9/12)	112,500 (30,000)	30,000	
Balance allocated (1:1)	82,500	41,250	41,250
	150,000	90,000	60,000

29 SALLY, BARRY, BILL AND BEA

Allocation of profit

	Total £	Sally £	Barry £	Bill £	Bea £
Period to 31 August 2015 (3 months) Interest on capital £80,000/£100,000/£200,000/£90,000 × 5% × 3/12	5,875	1,000	1,250	2,500	1,125
Balance (4:2:2:1)	183,125	81,389	40,695	40,694	20,347
(£756,000 × 3/12)	189,000				
Period to 31 May 2016 Balance (4:3:2:2) (£756,000 × 9/12)	567,000	206,182	154,636	103,091	103,091
	756,000	288,571	196,581	146,285	124,563

30 ALVIN, SIMON AND THEODORE

Allocation of profit

	Total £	Alvin £	Simon £	Theodore £
Period to: A = 31 July 2016 (£52,800 × 6/12)	B = 26,400			
Allocate (5:3:2)		C = 13,200	D = 7,920	E = 5,280
Period to: F = 31 January 2017 (£52,800 × 6/12)	G = 26,400			
Allocate (1:1)		H = 13,200	I = 13,200	
	52,800	26,400	21,120	5,280

31 SIAN AND ELLIE

Allocation of profit

	Total £	Sian £	Ellie £	Owen £
Period to: 30 April 2016 (£36,000 × 9/12)	27,000			
Allocate (2:1)		18,000	9,000	
Period to: 31 July 2016 (£36,000 × 3/12)	9,000			
Allocate (3:2:1)		4,500	3,000	1,500
	36,000	22,500	12,000	1,500
Year ended 31 July 2017 (3:2:1)	60,000	30,000	20,000	10,000

Owen: assessable profits

2016/17

	£
Profits from 1 May 2016 to 5 April 2017 (11 months)	
Period to 31 July 2016 (3 months)	1,500
8/12 of y/e 31 July 2017 (£10,000 × 8/12)	6,667
	8,167

2017/18

y/e 31 July 2017	10,000

Tutorial note

Partnership tax adjusted trading profits must be allocated between partners using the profit sharing arrangements of the accounting period. Once this is done the basis period rules can be applied to the profit shares of each partner to determine the taxable profits for the tax year.

Owen has just joined the partnership so opening year rules will apply to him as if he were a sole trader commencing on 1 May 2016 and preparing accounts to 31 July each year.

TRADING LOSSES

Key answer tips

The chief assessor has stated in the past that both theory and computational questions on losses seem to cause equal difficulty for learners. This is a surprise, as the expectation would be that computational questions would see a higher level of competence than theory based, but this is not the case. Learners appear to be quite confused over how losses can be relieved and show confusion over the different rules that apply to sole traders and limited companies. Since both might be seen in one task, it is very important to fully understand the rules and the connection between losses carried back, carried forward and relief in the year of the loss.

There is also evidence of learners providing incomplete answers, or simply answering a question as all true or all false, presumably as a quick guess at the answers. Unfortunately this method does not achieve good marks!

32 NICHOLAS

	True	False
A trading loss made by a company can only be offset against trading profits from the same trade when carrying the loss back		✓
A capital loss made by a company can be offset against trading profits in the year the loss is made and in future years		✓
A sole trader cannot restrict the amount of loss offset in the current year to preserve the personal allowance	✓	
A sole trader can carry forward a loss for a maximum of 4 years		✓

Tutorial note

1   *A company has three options for loss relief. It can offset trading losses:*

      –   *Against current year total profits only*

      –   *Against current year total profits and then carry back against total profits (i.e. cannot carry back unless the current year total profits have been relieved)*

      –   *Carry the loss forward against trading profits of the same trade.*

2   *Capital losses can only be set against capital gains and must be set against current year gains first. If any loss remains, it is then carried forward against future capital gains only.*

3   *A sole trader can carry forward a loss indefinitely but must agree the amount of the loss with HMRC within 4 years from the end of the tax year in which the loss arose.*

33 JOANNA

Answer = C

Tutorial note

A   *There is an option, but no obligation, to offset a sole trader's loss against total income in the current tax year.*

B   *A sole trader can offset trading losses against total income in the current tax year and/or prior year in any order. There is no requirement for the preceding year to be relieved first.*

C   *Correct answer.*

D   *Losses carried forward are set against trading profits only, not total income.*

34   STILTON LTD

(a)   £600

(b)   £10,200

(c)   £29,200

(d)   £Nil

(e)   C

(f)   A

Workings

Year ended 31 December	2016	2017
	£	£
Trading profit	8,000	Nil
Interest income	1,000	600
Chargeable gain	1,200	Nil
	———	———
Total profits	10,200	600
Less: Current year loss relief		(600)
Carry back 12 months	(10,200)	
	———	———
	Nil	Nil
Less: Qualifying charitable donation	(Wasted)	(Wasted)
	———	———
Taxable total profits	Nil	Nil
	———	———

Loss working

	£
Trading loss – year ended 31 December 2017	40,000
Less: Current year loss relief	(600)
Carry back relief – year ended 31 December 2016	(10,200)
	———
Loss to carry forward	29,200
	———

35   KANE

	True	False
A sole trader can offset a capital loss against chargeable gains in the current and/or the previous tax year, in any order		✓
Offset of current year capital losses is restricted to leave net gains equal to the annual exempt amount		✓
A sole trader can offset a trading loss against total income in the current and/or the previous tax year, in any order	✓	
For a trading loss made by a company to be relieved in the preceding accounting period, it must first have been relieved in the current accounting period	✓	
Use of trading loss relief by a company can result in wasted qualifying charitable donations	✓	

Tutorial note

1   *Capital losses can only be set against chargeable gains and must be set against current year gains first. If any loss remains, it is then carried forward against future chargeable gains only.*

2   *Current year capital losses must be set against current year gains and cannot be restricted to preserve an individual's annual exempt amount. However, the offset of capital losses brought forward is restricted to preserve an individual's annual exempt amount.*

36   GREEN LTD

(a)   D

(b)   (£180,000 – £175,000) = £5,000

(c)   (£30,000 – £20,000) = £10,000

(d)   £Nil

Workings

Year ended 31 March	2017
	£
Trading profit	175,000
Less: Trading loss relief b/f	(175,000)
	Nil
Interest income	30,000
Net chargeable gains (£20,000 – £20,000 capital loss b/f)	Nil
Total profits	30,000
Less: Qualifying charitable donation	(10,000)
Taxable total profits	20,000

CORPORATION TAX COMPUTATION

37 WITHERS LTD

	Accruals basis	Paid/Receipts basis
Qualifying charitable donations		✓
Trading income	✓	
Rental income	✓	
Interest income	✓	

38 MORGAN LTD

Answer = B

Tutorial note

A long period of account must be split into two chargeable accounting periods as follows:

CAP1:   First 12 months

CAP2:   Balance period.

39 LONG PERIOD OF ACCOUNT

	Time apportion	Separate computation	Period in which it arises
Chargeable gains			✓
Capital allowances		✓	
Trading profits	✓		
Qualifying charitable donations			✓

40   BROUSSE

	True	False
An individual sole trader with a fifteen month period ended 31 March 2017 will have a maximum AIA of £250,000 for capital allowance purposes	✓	
Where a car is provided to a director of a company, the director's private use of the car is not relevant when calculating capital allowances	✓	
An individual sole trader preparing a seventeen month period of account must calculate two separate capital allowances computations; one for the first 12 months and the second for the balancing period		✓
A company with a nine month accounting period ending on 31 March 2017 will qualify for a 75% (100% × 9/12) first year allowance in respect of the acquisition of a new low emission car		✓
An individual sole trader with an eleven month accounting period must time apportion the available FYAs by 11/12 for capital allowance purposes		✓
The maximum AIA for a sole trader business with an eight month accounting period ending 31 December 2016 is £133,333	✓	

Tutorial note

1   *The maximum AIA for a sole trader business with a fifteen month accounting period ending 31 March 2017 is £250,000 (£200,000 × 15/12).*

2   *The private use of assets provided by a company to its employees is ignored when calculating capital allowances.*

3   *A sole trader who prepares accounts for a 17 month period would prepare a single capital allowance computation for the whole period.*

4   *The first year allowance is not reduced where the accounting period is less than 12 months; it is always given in full.*

5   *FYAs are never time apportioned.*

6   *The maximum AIA for a sole trader business with an eight month accounting period ending 31 December 2016 is £133,333 (£200,000 × 8/12).*

41   TAXABLE TOTAL PROFITS

Answer = D

Tutorial note

Qualifying charitable donations are deductible on a paid basis.

Dividend income should be excluded from TTP.

Chargeable gains should be included in TTP.

Brought-forward losses are deductible from future trading profits arising from the same trade not TTP.

42   COUPE LTD

	Total	12 months to 30 Sept 2016	3 months to 31 Dec 2016
	£	£	£
Trading income	15,750	12,600	3,150
Capital allowances	7,000	5,000	2,000
Rental income	7,500	6,000	1,500
Interest income	3,000	2,400	600
Chargeable gain	800	800	Nil
Qualifying charitable donation	1,000	Nil	1,000

Tutorial note

Trading income and rental income are time apportioned.

Separate computations for each chargeable accounting period are required for capital allowances.

Interest income is allocated on an accruals basis.

Chargeable gains are allocated according to date of disposal and qualifying charitable donations according to the date of payment.

43   MERCURY LTD

Corporation tax payable – 9 months ended 31 March 2017

	£
Trading profit	250,000
Less: Trading loss relief b/f	(35,000)
	215,000
Net chargeable gains (£13,000 – £13,000 capital loss b/f)	Nil
Total profits	215,000
Less: Qualifying charitable donation	(2,000)
Taxable total profits	213,000
Corporation tax liability at 20%	42,600

44   PANGOLIN LTD

Corporation tax payable – 16 month period ended 31 March 2017

	Year ended 30 November 2016	Four months ended 31 March 2017
	£	£
Trading profit (12:4)	60,000	20,000
Rental income (12:4)	16,500	5,500
Chargeable gain (note)	61,000	–
Total profits	137,500	25,500
Less: Qualifying charitable donation	(3,000)	–
Taxable total profits	134,500	25,500
Corporation tax liability at 20%	26,900	5,100

The total corporation tax liability is £32,000

Tutorial note

The capital loss arose in the four month period ended 31 March 2017. It cannot be deducted from the chargeable gain of the previous accounting period. It must be carried forward for relief in the future.

CHARGEABLE GAINS

EXEMPT ASSETS

45   DEBREL

	Chargeable asset	Exempt asset
Dishwasher – sold for £300		✓
Diamond bracelet – sold for £4,000 (cost £2,500)		✓
Jaguar car – sold for £70,000		✓
Exchequer stock – sold for £100,000		✓

46   BIRCH

	Chargeable asset	Exempt asset
Antique vase – sold for £23,000	✓	
Vintage classic car		✓
Unquoted shares	✓	

47   ROSE

	Chargeable asset	Exempt asset
Holiday cottage	✓	
Quoted shares in an ISA		✓
Racehorse (wasting chattel)		✓

48   LARCH

	Chargeable asset	Exempt asset
Freehold factory	✓	
Diamond necklace – sold for £17,000	✓	
Racing pigeon (wasting chattel)		✓

49   ARKWRIGHT

	Chargeable asset	Exempt asset
Quoted shares	✓	
Prize winning greyhound (wasting chattel)		✓
Painting by Monet – sold for £300,000	✓	

CHARGEABLE GAIN COMPUTATIONS

Key answer tips

The chief assessor has pointed out in the past that connected persons are an area that appears to cause problems. You may be tested both on who is connected and what the impact of that connection is and must be able to demonstrate an understanding of this.

There is also evidence that learners are struggling with indexation allowance and how to apply it accurately. In particular look out for the different presentation of some indexation information in the questions which are shown in some of the shares questions in the next section.

50 CHARGEABLE GAIN COMPUTATIONS

	Applies to companies only	Applies to individuals only	Applies to both companies and individuals
(a) Annual exempt amount		✓	
(b) Indexation allowance	✓		
(c) Rollover relief			✓
(d) Entrepreneurs' relief		✓	

51 WENDY

	True	False
Indexation allowance cannot create an allowable capital loss for companies	✓	
Indexation allowance can create an allowable capital loss for individuals		✓
The indexation factor is calculated to two decimal places		✓
The indexation factor is calculated using the movement in the retail prices index from the month of acquisition to the month of disposal	✓	
Indexation allowance is calculated for bonus issues in the share pool of a company		✓

Tutorial note

Indexation allowance cannot create nor increase a loss.

It is only available to companies, not individuals.

The indexation factor must be calculated to three decimal places, unless within the share pool.

Indexation is not required before recording a bonus issue, but is required before recording a rights issue.

52 SYLVESTER LTD

Allowable loss computation

	£
Deemed sale proceeds	6,000
Less: Cost	(10,000)
	(4,000)
Less: Indexation allowance	(Nil)
Allowable loss	(4,000)

Tutorial note

Where a non-wasting chattel is sold for less than £6,000, but cost more than £6,000; an allowable loss is available. However, the loss is restricted to the loss that would arise if the gross sale proceeds are deemed to be £6,000.

Indexation allowance cannot increase an allowable loss.

53 REST LTD

Answer = B

Working:

Chargeable gain computation

	£
Sale proceeds	8,000
Less: Cost	(3,000)
Unindexed gain	5,000
Less: Indexation allowance (£3,000 × 0.243)	(729)
Chargeable gain	4,271
Chargeable gain cannot exceed: 5/3 × (£8,000 − £6,000)	3,333

Tutorial note

Where a non-wasting chattel is sold for more than £6,000 and it cost less than £6,000; a normal chargeable gain computation is required.

However, the gain cannot exceed the 5/3rd rule as shown above.

54 XYZ LTD

Chargeable gain computation

	£
Sale proceeds	250,000
Less: Cost	(100,000)
Extension	(22,000)
	————
Unindexed gain	128,000
Less: Indexation allowance	
(£100,000 × 0.291)	(29,100)
(£22,000 × 0.127)	(2,794)
	————
Chargeable gain	96,106
	————

Tutorial note

Roof repairs are not capital and cannot be deducted in the capital gains calculation.

Improvement costs such as the extension must be indexed separately. Indexation runs from the month in which the costs were incurred.

55 LIVINGSTONE LTD

Chargeable gain computation

	£
Sale proceeds	200,000
Less: Cost £180,000 × £200,000/(£200,000 + £700,000)	(40,000)
	————
Unindexed gain	160,000
Less: Indexation allowance (£40,000 × 0.600)	(24,000)
	————
Chargeable gain	136,000
	————

Tutorial note

The allowable cost in a part disposal computation is calculated using:

A/A+B   where   A = market value of the part sold

B = the market value of the remainder

56 STAN

	True	False
An individual disposing of one third of his investment land must compare one third of the original cost of the land to the sale proceeds received to calculate the chargeable gain		✓
A company is 100% owned by Mr Black. The company gifts a capital asset to Mr Black's wife. The gift will be a nil gain/nil loss disposal for capital gains purposes		✓
Stan is connected to his mother, brother, sister-in-law and niece for the purposes of capital gains tax		✓
Meera owns a painting which cost £12,000 in 2000. She gives it to a charity in 2016 when the painting is worth £50,000. She has a chargeable gain of £38,000		✓
Fred bought shares in July 2010 costing £17,500. If Fred dies in 2017 when the shares are worth £40,000, his estate will be charged capital gains tax on a gain of £22,500		✓

Tutorial note

Only gifts between husband and wife or between civil partners are made at no gain no loss. A gift from a company cannot be a no gain no loss disposal.

Stan is not connected to his niece.

Gifts to charity and disposals on death are exempt disposals.

57 TOPHAM LTD

Chargeable gain computation

	£
Sale proceeds	42,000
Less: Cost	(40,000)
	2,000
Less: Indexation allowance	
(£40,000 × 0.082) = £3,280 restricted as cannot create a loss	(2,000)
Chargeable gain	Nil

Tutorial note

Indexation allowance cannot create an allowable loss.

58   SYBILE

Chargeable gain computation

	£
Sale proceeds	160,000
Less: Cost £560,000 × £160,000/(£160,000 + £840,000)	(89,600)
	70,400
Less: Indexation allowance (not applicable for individuals)	(Nil)
Chargeable gain	70,400

59   RIZWAN

	True	False
On the disposal of a non-wasting chattel with gross sale proceeds in excess of £6,000 and cost of less than £6,000, the chargeable gain is calculated using deemed sale proceeds of £6,000		✓
Wasting chattels are exempt if disposed of by individuals or companies	✓	
On the disposal of a non-wasting chattel with gross sale proceeds in excess of £6,000 and cost of less than £6,000, the chargeable gain cannot exceed: 5/3 × (gross sale proceeds – £6,000)	✓	
On the disposal of a non-wasting chattel at a loss with gross sale proceeds and cost in excess of £6,000, the allowable loss is calculated using deemed sale proceeds of £6,000		✓

Tutorial note

The deemed sale proceeds of £6,000 are only used when a non-wasting chattel is sold at a loss; where the sale proceeds are less than £6,000 and the cost is in excess of £6,000.

Therefore, it is not applicable in the first scenario, which is a sale at a gain.

It is not applicable in the last scenario as both the cost and sale proceeds exceed £6,000. A normal allowable loss is calculated in this situation.

60 KAREN, BEN AND SARAH

(a) **Karen**

Net chargeable gain before annual exempt amount

	£
Chargeable gains in the year (£5,000 + £7,000)	12,000
Less: Allowable capital losses in the year	(4,000)
Net chargeable gains before annual exempt amount	8,000

Tutorial note

Current year capital losses must be offset against current year gains, even if that brings the net chargeable gain below the annual exempt amount. The offset cannot be restricted to preserve the annual exempt amount.

(b) **Ben**

Net chargeable gain before annual exempt amount

	£
Chargeable gains in the year (£9,000 + £3,600)	12,600
Less: Allowable capital losses in the year	(Nil)
	12,600
Less: Allowable capital losses b/f	(1,500)
Net chargeable gain before annual exempt amount	11,100

Tutorial note

Brought forward capital losses are restricted to preserve the annual exempt amount.

(c) **Sarah**

Net chargeable gain before annual exempt amount

	£
Residential property	
£9,900 (£23,000 − £2,000 − £11,100) × 18%	1,782.00
Plot of land	
£7,000 × 10%	700.00
	2,482.00

Tutorial note

The capital loss and the annual exempt amount are deducted from the gain on the residential property in priority to other gains.

Sarah has £22,000 (£32,000 – £10,000) of unused basic rate band available. Therefore her gains both fall in the basic rate band and are taxed at 18% or 10%.

DISPOSAL OF SHARES

Key answer tips

Share disposals are commonly tested. The most commonly recurring error is the handling of matching rules where shares are bought 30 days after a disposal (for individuals) or 9 days before (for companies). It is common for learners to ignore the matching rules completely and simply show one large pool that takes events in strict chronological order.

61 PUCK LTD

Chargeable gain computation

	£
Sale proceeds	24,000
Less: Cost (W)	(14,000)
Unindexed gain	10,000
Less: Indexation allowance (W) (£17,878 – £14,000)	(3,878)
Chargeable gain	6,122

Working: Share pool

	Number of shares	Cost £	Indexed cost £
June 2006	3,000	12,000	12,000
January 2010			
Bonus issue (1 for 3)	1,000	Nil	Nil
	4,000	12,000	12,000
December 2013			
Indexation update (£12,000 × 0.277)			3,324
Rights issue (1 for 4) @ £2	1,000	2,000	2,000
	5,000	14,000	17,324
April 2016			
Indexation update (£17,324 × 0.032)			554
	5,000	14,000	17,878
Disposal	(5,000)	(14,000)	(17,878

Tutorial note

Indexation is not required before recording a bonus issue, but is required before recording a rights issue and the disposal.

Take care when reading the indexation information if it is presented in a table as in this question – you simply need to look up the row and column of the two dates and take the indexation factor from the relevant box – there is no need to do any calculations to establish the indexation factor.

62 PISTON LTD

Chargeable gain computation

	£
Sale proceeds	18,800
Less: Cost (W)	(17,770)
Unindexed gain	1,030
Less: Indexation allowance (W) (£22,707 – £17,770)	
Restricted, indexation allowance cannot create a loss	(1,030)
Chargeable gain	Nil

Working: Share pool

	Number of shares	Cost £	Indexed cost £
August 2004	2,700	10,640	10,640
July 2011			
Bonus issue (1 for 3)	900	Nil	Nil
	3,600	10,640	10,640
January 2012			
Indexation update (£10,640 × 0.270)			2,873
Acquisition	2,300	7,130	7,130
	5,900	17,770	20,643
May 2016			
Indexation update (£20,643 × 0.100)			2,064
			22,707
Disposal	(5,900)	(17,770)	(22,707)
Balance c/f	Nil	Nil	Nil

Tutorial note

Indexation is not required before recording a bonus issue, but is required before recording the disposal.

Indexation allowance cannot turn a chargeable gain into a capital loss (or increase a capital loss).

63   DREAM LTD

Chargeable gain computation

	£
Sale proceeds	43,000
Less: Cost (W)	(9,333)
Unindexed gain	33,667
Less: Indexation allowance (W) (£15,363 – £9,333)	(6,030)
Chargeable gain	27,637

Working: Share pool

	Number of shares	Cost £	Indexed cost £
March 1998	6,000	12,000	12,000
June 2003			
Bonus issue (1 for 2)	3,000	Nil	Nil
	9,000	12,000	12,000
December 2016			
Indexation update (£12,000 × 0.646)			7,752
	9,000	12,000	19,752
Disposal	(7,000)		
(7,000/9,000) × £12,000 and £19,752		(9,333)	(15,363)
Balance c/f	2,000	2,667	4,389

Tutorial note

Indexation is not required before recording a bonus issue, but is required before recording the disposal.

Take care when reading the indexation information if it is presented in a table as in this question – you simply need to look up the row and column of the two dates and take the indexation factor from the relevant box – there is no need to do any calculations to establish the indexation factor.

64   BATMAN LTD

Chargeable gain computation

	£
Sale proceeds (5,000 × £5)	25,000
Less: Cost (W)	(9,907)
Unindexed gain	15,093
Less: Indexation allowance (W) (£13,407 – £9,907)	(3,500)
Chargeable gain	11,593

Working: Share pool

	Number of shares	Cost £	Indexed cost £
May 2004	7,000	14,000	14,000
July 2006			
Bonus issue (1 for 8)	875	Nil	Nil
	7,875	14,000	14,000
July 2010			
Indexation update (£14,000 × 0.199)			2,786
Rights issue (1 for 5) @ £3	1,575	4,725	4,725
	9,450	18,725	21,511
September 2016			
Indexation update (£21,511 × 0.178)			3,829
	9,450	18,725	25,340
Disposal	(5,000)		
(5,000/9,450) × £18,725 and £25,340		(9,907)	(13,407)
Balance c/f	4,450	8,818	11,933

Tutorial note

Indexation is not required before recording a bonus issue, but is required before recording the rights issue and the disposal.

65   SHELBYVILLE LTD

Chargeable gain computation

(1)   Disposal of 2,000 shares matched with the January 2016 purchase (in previous 9 days)

		£
Sale proceeds (2,000 × £3.20)		6,400
Less: Cost		(5,950)
Chargeable gain		450

(2)   Disposal of 3,875 shares from the pool

		£
Sale proceeds (3,875 × £3.20)		12,400
Less: Cost (W)		(8,809)
Unindexed gain		3,591
Less: Indexation allowance (W) (£9,046 – £8,809)		(237)
Chargeable gain		3,354
Total gains (£150 + £3,354)		3,804

Working: Share pool

	Number of shares	Cost £	Indexed cost £
May 2015 Purchase	10,000	23,300	23,300
November 2015 Bonus issue (1 for 40)	250	Nil	Nil
	10,250	23,300	23,300
February 2017 Indexation update (£23,300 × 0.027)			629
	10,250	23,300	23,929
Disposal	(3,875)		
(3,875/10,250) × £23,300 and £23,929		(8,809)	(9,046)
Balance c/f	6,375	14,491	14,883

Tutorial note

The matching rules for a company specify that disposals of shares are matched with:

1   *purchases on the same day, and then*

2   *purchases in the previous 9 days (LIFO basis), and then*

3   *shares held in the share pool.*

No indexation is given for shares matched with purchases on the same day or previous 9 days. Indexation is not required before recording a bonus issue, but is required before recording the disposal.

66   JAMES

Chargeable gain computation

	£
Sale proceeds (550 × £14.20)	7,810
Less: Cost (W)	(2,250)
Chargeable gain	5,560

Working: Share pool

	Number of shares	Cost £
July 2007	1,000	4,500
August 2009		
Bonus issue (1 for 10)	100	Nil
	1,100	4,500
October 2016 – Disposal	(550)	
(550/1,100) × £4,500		(2,250)
Balance c/f	550	2,250

Tutorial note

Indexation allowance is not given to an individual.

67   GOODWIN

Chargeable gain computation

(1)   Disposal of 800 shares matched with the February 2017 purchase (in next 30 days)

	£
Sale proceeds (800 × £9.00)	7,200
Less: Cost	(6,800)
Chargeable gain	400

(2)   Disposal of 1,700 shares from the pool

	£
Sale proceeds (1,700 × £9.00)	15,300
Less: Cost (W)	(8,925)
Chargeable gain	6,375
Total gains (£400 + £6,375)	6,775

Working: Share pool

	Number of shares	Cost £
March 2010	3,600	25,200
July 2011		
Bonus issue (1 for 3)	1,200	Nil
	4,800	25,200
January 2017 – Disposal	(1,700)	
(1,700/4,800) × £25,200		(8,925)
Balance c/f	3,100	16,275

Tutorial note

Remember to match shares sold with those acquired in the next 30 days before matching with those in the share pool.

CAPITAL GAINS – RELIEFS

Key answer tips

Historically learners have performed badly in these areas. A common question is capital losses and in particular their interaction with the annual exempt amount. An area that learners are clearly struggling with is the capital gains tax payable by individual, using information provided regarding their taxable income. You will need to calculate the remaining basic rate band available to set against the taxable gains, before applying tax at the appropriate rates. However, take care when reading the question as it may only ask for the chargeable gain which is taxable at 10%/18% and 20%/28%, which means it is not necessary to actually calculate the tax itself. Also take care to identify whether the annual exempt amount has already been deducted from the figures provided or not.

68 SUSAN AND RACHEL

(a) A

Tutorial note

Rollover relief is available where an individual or a company

- *disposes of a qualifying business asset, and*
- *replaces it with another qualifying business asset*
- *within 12 months before, and*
- *36 months after the date of disposal.*

(b) C

Tutorial note

Entrepreneurs' relief is available as Susan has made a qualifying disposal and she has owned the business for at least one year.

The annual exempt amount is deducted from the antique table gain first, leaving all of the business gain to be charged to tax. The remaining gain is then taxed at 10% as entrepreneurs' relief is available.

The business gain must be taxed first, before the antique table gain, to use up any remaining basic rate band (if applicable).

The antique table gain, after the annual exempt amount, is therefore taxed at 20% as Susan is a higher rate taxpayer.

(c) B

Tutorial note

Capital losses can only be set against chargeable gains, not any other income.

Current year capital losses must be set against chargeable gains of the same tax year. Any losses remaining are carried forward for offset against future chargeable gains.

(d) D

Tutorial note

Disposals to a connected person (e.g. brother) are treated as if disposed of for their full market value at the time of the transfer.

69 MALCOLM AND JEREMY

(a) £240,000

Working:

Chargeable gain computation

	£
Sale proceeds	725,000
Less: Cost	(350,000)
Chargeable gain	375,000

Chargeable at time of disposal = Lower of

(i) Chargeable gain = £375,000

(ii) Sale proceeds not reinvested = (£725,000 – £590,000) = £135,000

i.e. £135,000

Rollover relief is therefore the remaining gain:

(£375,000 – £135,000) = £240,000

(b) A = 1 September 2015

B = 1 September 2019

Tutorial note

Rollover relief is available where an individual or a company

- *disposes of a qualifying business asset, and*

- *replaces with another qualifying business asset*

- *within 12 months before, and*

- *36 months after the date of disposal.*

If all of the sale proceeds are reinvested, the whole of the chargeable gain can be deferred.

If not all of the sale proceeds are reinvested, the chargeable gain now is the lower of the

(i) chargeable gain, or

(ii) sale proceeds not reinvested.

The remaining gain can be deferred with a rollover relief claim.

---

70 AVAILABILITY OF RELIEFS

Answer = C is false

---

71 OLIVER LTD

Answer = C

Working:

Chargeable at time of disposal = Lower of

(i)   Chargeable gain = £300,000

(ii) Sale proceeds not reinvested = (£800,000 – £750,000) = £50,000

i.e. £50,000

Rollover relief is therefore the remaining gain:

(£300,000 – £50,000) = £250,000

Tutorial note

A   A claim must be made for rollover relief, it is not automatic.

B   Shares are not qualifying assets for the purposes of rollover relief.

C   Correct answer.

D   The time limit for reinvestment expires in May 2019; therefore a purchase in June 2019 is too late to qualify.

72 JOHN, PAUL, GEORGE AND RINGO

(a)   D

Tutorial note

A   Rollover relief is not available on disposals of shares.

B   John must work for the company for these shares to be eligible for entrepreneurs' relief.

C   The shares are sold for their full market value and therefore there is no gift element in the transaction.

(b)   D

Tutorial note

A   Rollover relief is only available on disposals of qualifying business assets, not vases. It is also not available on gifts.

B   Entrepreneurs' relief is only available on the disposal of qualifying business assets, not antique vases.

C   Gift relief is only available on the disposal of qualifying business assets, not antique vases.

(c)   C

Tutorial note

A   Rollover relief is not available on disposals of shares.

B   Entrepreneurs' relief is only available on shares if the individual owns at least 5% of the shares and works for the company.

C   Gift relief is available on the sale at undervaluation of a qualifying business asset, which includes unquoted trading company shares.

(d)   B

Tutorial note

A   Rollover relief is not available if there is no reinvestment of sale proceeds in qualifying business assets.

B   Entrepreneurs' relief is available on the sale of a partnership interest.

C   The partnership interest is sold for full market value and therefore there is no gift element in the transaction.

73   NORMAN

(a)   £68,900

Working:

	£
Chargeable gain on the business	700,000
Less: Annual exempt amount	(11,100)
Taxable gain	688,900
Capital gains tax @ 10%	68,890

(b)   31 January 2019

(i.e. 12 months from 31 January following the end of the tax year in which the disposal occurred)

74   HARRY AND BRIONY

(a)   D

Tutorial note

A   *Rollover relief is not available on disposals of shares.*

B   *If not all the sale proceeds are reinvested, the chargeable gain now is the **lower** of the*

   (i)   *chargeable gain, and*

   (ii)   *sale proceeds not reinvested.*

   *The **remaining gain** can be deferred with a rollover relief claim.*

C   *When rollover relief is claimed, the gain is rolled over by **deducting** the gain from the base cost of the replacement asset.*

(b)   A

Working:

Capital gains tax – 2016/17

	£
Gain on business	5,500,000
Less: Annual exempt amount	(11,100)
Taxable gain	5,488,900
Gains qualifying for entrepreneurs' relief	
(£10,000,000 lifetime allowance – £4,900,000 used in 2015/16)	
= £5,100,000 × 10%	510,000
Remaining gain (£5,488,900 – £5,100,000) = £388,900 × 20%	77,780
	587,780

(c)   C

(d)   C

Tutorial note

Disposals between husband and wife are treated as 'no gain/no loss' transactions.

The market value of the asset at the date of transfer is irrelevant; the recipient spouse takes over the asset at its original cost.

The deemed disposal value of the asset is therefore the cost to the original spouse, and this is also the deemed cost for the recipient spouse.

75   **CHERYL**

(a)   C

(b)   C

Tutorial note

Disposals between husband and wife or civil partners are treated as 'no gain / no loss' transactions.

The market value of the asset at the date of transfer is irrelevant; the recipient takes over the asset at its original cost.

The deemed disposal value of the asset is therefore the cost to the original spouse, and this is also the deemed cost for the recipient spouse.

James makes the disposal for £120,000 and will have a gain of £70,000. He may deduct his own annual exempt amount from this gain but unused annual exempt amounts cannot be transferred between individuals.

Disposing of assets through a spouse or civil partner can be advantageous. The couple will save tax if they have unused annual exempt amount, unused basic rate band or unused capital losses to set against the gain.

(c)   A

76   **ALLYN AND SIMON**

(a)   £600,000

Working:

Chargeable gain computation

	£
Sale proceeds	2,850,000
Less: Cost	(1,400,000)
Chargeable gain	1,450,000

Chargeable at time of disposal = Lower of

(i)   Chargeable gain = £1,450,000

(ii)   Sale proceeds not reinvested = (£2,850,000 – £2,000,000) = £850,000

i.e. £850,000

Rollover relief is therefore the remaining gain:

(£1,450,000 – £850,000) = £600,000

(b)   A = 1 February 2014

B = 1 February 2018

Tutorial note

Rollover relief is available where an individual or company

- disposes of a qualifying business asset, and
- replaces with another qualifying business asset
- within 12 months before, and
- 36 months after the date of disposal.

If all of the sale proceeds are reinvested, the whole of the chargeable gain can be deferred.

If not all of the sale proceeds are reinvested, the chargeable gain now is the lower of the

(i)   chargeable gain, and

(ii)   sale proceeds not reinvested.

The remaining gain can be deferred with a rollover relief claim.

77   EVAN, ZAK AND LILIA

Taxpayer	Taxable income	Chargeable gain	
		18% CGT	**28% CGT**
	£	£	£
Evan	21,500	10,500	98,400
Zak	29,700	2,300	106,600
Lilia	42,300	0	108,900

Tutorial note

Capital gains tax is charged at 18% and 28% on gains in respect of the disposal of residential property.

The chargeable gains provided in the question are before the deduction of the annual exempt amount. The taxable gains in each case are therefore £108,900 (£120,000 – £11,100).

The amount of the chargeable gain taxable at 18% is calculated by deducting the taxable income from the basic rate band available of £32,000.

78   OPHELIA, GEORGIA AND SID

Taxpayer	Taxable income	Chargeable gain	
		10% CGT	**20% CGT**
	£	£	£
Ophelia	35,000	0	12,000
Georgia	21,200	10,800	1,200
Sid	16,850	12,000	0

Tutorial note

In this question you are provided with taxable gains after the deduction of the annual exempt amount. It is therefore not necessary to deduct the AEA – always take care when reading the question to ensure you understand the information provided.

The amount of the chargeable gain taxable at 10% is calculated by deducting the taxable income from the basic rate band available of £32,000.

NATIONAL INSURANCE CONTRIBUTIONS

SELF-EMPLOYED INDIVIDUALS

Key answer tips

Calculating the NICs payable by partners causes learners the most difficulty. Remember that it may be necessary to apportion partnership profits before calculating the class 4 NICs and that each partner will be liable to their own class 2 NICs.

79   JENNY AND JACK

(a)   **Class 4 NICs**

	£ p
(£43,000 – £8,060) = £34,940 × 9%	3,144.60
(£85,000 – £43,000) = £42,000 × 2%	840.00
	3,984.60

(b)   **Class 2 NICs**

	£ p
(£2.80 × 52 weeks)	145.60

(c)   C

Tutorial note

Self-employed taxpayers pay class 4 NICs based on their taxable trading profits in excess of £8,060 and the fixed rate class 2 NICs of £2.80 per week provided taxable trading profits exceed £5,965.

80   CARTER

Answer = C

Tutorial note

Self-employed taxpayers pay class 4 NICs based on their taxable trading profits in excess of £8,060 and the fixed rate class 2 NICs of £2.80 per week provided taxable trading profits exceed £5,965.

The taxable trading profit for the year ended 31 December 2016, which is taxed in 2016/17, is below the class 4 threshold of £8,060 but above the class 2 threshold of £5,965. Therefore there is no liability to class 4 NICs but there is a liability to class 2 NICs.

81   IVOR

(a)   **Amount liable to class 4 NICs at 9%**

(£43,000 – £8,060)   £34,940

(b)   **Amount liable to class 4 NICs at 2%**

(£100,000 – £43,000)   £57,000

(c)   **Class 2 NICs**

£ p

(£2.80 × 52 weeks)   145.60

(d)   **True or false**

	True	False
Ivor will also be required to pay class 1 Primary NICs in relation to his salary from the partnership		✓

Tutorial note

Class 1 primary NICs are paid by employees. Self-employed individuals pay class 4 on their profits regardless of when those profits are drawn from the business.

82   JAKE, SUE AND PETE

(a)   **Class 2 NICs**

	£ p
(£2.80 × 52 weeks)	145.60

(b)   **Class 4 NICs**

	£ p
(£41,000 – £8,060) = £32,940 × 9%	2,964.60

(c)   £Nil

Tutorial note

Self-employed taxpayers pay class 4 NICs based on their taxable trading profits in excess of £8,060 and the fixed rate class 2 NICs of £2.80 per week provided taxable trading profits exceed £5,965.

83   THOMAS AND SUZANNE

(a)   **Amount liable to class 4 NICs at 9%**

Thomas is past state pension age	£Nil

(h)   **Class 4 NICs**

	£ p
(£35,000 – £8,060) = £26,940 × 9%	2,424.60

(c)   D

Tutorial note

Self-employed taxpayers pay class 4 NICs based on their taxable trading profits in excess of £8,060 and the fixed rate class 2 NICs of £2.80 per week provided taxable trading profits exceed £5,965.

However, if the taxpayer has reached state pension age by the start of the tax year they have no class 4 liability.

84 AMELIE AND ALEXANDER

(a) **Class 4 NICs payable by Amelie**

	£ p
Share of partnership profits	
(£75,000 - £5,000) × 60%	42,000
(£42,000 – £8,060) = £33,940 × 9%	3,054.60

(b) **Class 4 NICs payable by Alexander**

	£ p
Share of partnership profits	
£5,000 + ((£75,000 – £5,000) × 40%)	33,000
(£33,000 – £8,060) = £24,940 × 9%	2,244.60

(c) **Class 2 NICs payable by Amelie**

	£ p
(£2.80 × 52 weeks)	145.60

Tutorial note

When calculating NICs for partners you must first apportion the partnership profits between the partners following the normal partnership rules. You should then apply the normal NIC rules to those apportioned profits, not the partnership 'salary'.

Class 2 NICs are payable by all partners in full.

CURRENT TAX RELIEFS AND OTHER TAX ISSUES

R&D TAX CREDITS AND IR35

85 BARRY

	True	False
Ellis plc is a SME. They have already deducted £40,000 of qualifying research and development cost from their profits. They can deduct a further £92,000 in arriving at their adjusted trading profit.		✓
Jade plc has annual turnover below 100 million euros. It is automatically classed as an SME.		✓
The cost of heating and lighting a research and development department can never be part of the qualifying cost for R&D tax credits.		✓

86 CAITLIN

	True	False
Employers' NIC for staff involved in research and development activities can be part of the qualifying cost for R&D tax credits.	✓	
If a SME makes a loss due to qualifying research and development expenditure they must surrender the loss in return for a cash payment.		✓
Capital expenditure of £50,000 is incurred by a SME on qualifying research and development projects. The company can claim capital allowances on £115,000 (£50,000 × 230%).		✓

Tutorial note

If a loss is incurred due to R&D then it may be surrendered in return for a cash payment. It is not compulsory to do this.

Capital expenditure does not qualify for R&D tax credits.

87 JOE

	True	False
All the turnover of a personal service company (PSC) is automatically subject to a deemed employment income tax charge.		✓
IR35 legislation exists to prevent a PSC from being used to disguise permanent employment.	✓	
If a PSC has only one client it is an indication that this is a disguised employment.	✓	
If a PSC has several clients then none of its income will be subject to a deemed employment income charge.		✓

Tutorial note

A personal service company is subject to the IR35 rules where the relationship between the worker and the client would be considered to be an employment relationship if the existence of the PSC was ignored.

It is possible for a PSC to have several clients and for the IR35 rules only to apply to one or two of them. These are called relevant engagements.

In order to decide if a contract is a relevant engagement a number of factors must be considered. If a PSC only has one client then this is indicative of an employment relationship but is not conclusive on its own. Conversely if a PSC has several clients this is not a guarantee that the IR35 rules will not apply.

88   IRIS

	True	False
Central plc engages Zoom Ltd to provide some consultancy services. Zoom Ltd is a PSC. If the contract between Central plc and Zoom Ltd is deemed to be a relevant engagement under IR35 rules then Central plc must deduct income tax and NIC from the payments made to Zoom Ltd.		✓
If the owner of a PSC provides their own tools and equipment in carrying out a contract for a client then that contract cannot be deemed to be a relevant engagement subject to IR35 rules.		✓
If the owner of a PSC cannot send a substitute to carry out work for a client but must perform the work themselves, then that is an indication that the contract may be deemed to be a relevant engagement subject to IR35 rules.	✓	

Tutorial note

The client company is not subject to the IR35 rules. It is Zoom Ltd that would be subject to an employment income charge. This requires Zoom Ltd to treat the payments from Central plc as if they were a salary paid out at the end of the tax year. Zoom Ltd must deduct tax and NIC and pay employers' NIC on the deemed salary, although normal employment expenses can be deducted.

Providing own tools and equipment is an indication that the relationship is not a disguised employment but is not conclusive on its own.

A requirement to perform work personally is an indication that that the relationship is a disguised employment, although it is not conclusive on its own.

SELF-ASSESSMENT

PAYMENT DATES

Key answer tips

When asked for dates it is important to state the full date, including the year, and to ensure that it is the right year! Unfortunately, if one date is wrong, they tend to all be wrong.

When calculating payments on account, you must remember which year the payments should be based on, ensure that you know what is included in the payments on account system and what is payable as part of the balancing payment. You should ensure that you state accurate dates.

89 INDIVIDUAL'S PAYMENT DATES

(a)   31 January 2017

(b)   31 January 2018

(c)   31 January 2018

(d)   31 July 2017

Tutorial note

A self-employed individual must pay 'Payments on account' for income tax and class 4 NICs, based on the previous year's income tax and class 4 NICs payable, on 31 January in the tax year and 31 July following the end of the tax year.

The final balancing payment is due on 31 January following the end of the tax year.

Capital gains tax is never paid in instalments, it is all due on 31 January following the end of the tax year.

90 PAYMENTS ON ACCOUNT (POAs)

	True	False
POAs are not required if the income tax payable for the previous year by self-assessment is less than £1,000	✓	
POAs for 2016/17 are due on 31 July 2017 and 31 January 2018		✓
POAs are not required if more than 80% of the income tax and capital gains tax liability for the previous year was met through tax deducted under PAYE		✓
POAs of class 2 NICs are never required	✓	
POAs of class 4 NICs are optional; the taxpayer can choose to pay under monthly direct debit or quarterly invoice if they prefer		✓

Tutorial note

POAs are not required if:

(i) *the total amount of income tax and class 4 NICs payable for the previous year after the deduction of tax under PAYE is less than £1,000; or*

(ii) *more than 80% of the income tax and class 4 NICs liability for the previous year was met through tax deducted at source.*

Capital gains tax is not taken into account when deciding whether POAs are required.

POAs are not optional. Unless the conditions above apply, POAs must be paid.

POAs are due on 31 January in the tax year (i.e. 31 January 2017) and 31 July following the end of the tax year (i.e. 31 July 2017) for 2016/17.

91   COMPANY PAYMENT DATES

(a) 14 October 2016

(b) 1 October 2017

(c) 1 November 2017

(d) 14 October 2017

Tutorial note

(a) *The augmented profits limit of £1,500,000 is divided by two for the total number of 51% group companies (company plus one 51% group company). With a revised limit of £750,000 and augmented profits of £800,000, the company is 'large'. As it was also 'large' in the previous year it must pay its tax under the quarterly instalment rules. The first payment is due on 14th of the 7th month following the start of the chargeable accounting period.*

(b) *With an augmented profits limit of £1,125,000 (£1,500,000 × 9/12) for the short accounting period and augmented profits of £800,000, the company is not 'large'. The due date for its tax liability is 9 months and one day after the end of the chargeable accounting period.*

(c) *With an augmented profits limit of £1,500,000 and augmented profits of £800,000, the company is not 'large'. The due date for its tax liability is 9 months and one day after the end of the chargeable accounting period.*

(d) *With an augmented profits limit of £437,500 (£1,500,000 ÷ 2 × 7/12) and augmented profits of £800,000, the company is 'large'. As it was also large in the previous year it must pay its tax under the quarterly instalment rules. The first payment is always due on 14th of the 7th month following the start of the chargeable accounting period, regardless of the length of the accounting period.*

92 DUE DATES

(a) 31 July 2017

(b) 31 October 2017

(c) 1 October 2017

(d) Large/Current

Tutorial note

A self-employed individual must pay 'payments on account' for income tax and class 4 NICs based on the previous years' income tax payable and class 4 liability on:

(i)   31 January in the tax year, and

(ii)   31 July following the end of the tax year.

An individual can choose to file their return either on paper or electronically online:

(i)   If filing on paper, the due date is 31 October following the end of the tax year.

(ii)   Electronic filing must be submitted by 31 January following the end of the tax year.

The normal due date for corporation tax is 9 months and one day after the end of the chargeable accounting period.

However, where the company is 'large' (i.e. its augmented profits exceed the £1,500,000 augmented profits limit), it must pay its corporation tax by quarterly instalments based on the estimated corporation tax liability for the current year.

93 COMPANY DUE DATES

(a) 31 March 2018

(b) 1 January 2018

(c) 14 October 2016

(d) 14 July 2017

Tutorial note

The normal due date for corporation tax is 9 months and one day after the end of the chargeable accounting period.

However, where the company is large (i.e. has augmented profits above £1,500,000), it must pay its corporation tax by quarterly instalments.

The instalments are due on the 14th day of the 7th, 10th, 13th and 16th month after the start of the chargeable accounting period.

ADMINISTRATION, PENALTIES AND ETHICAL STANDARDS

Key answer tips

As stated before, when asked for dates it is important to state the full date, including the year, and to ensure that it is the right year! It is not possible to gain full marks here without applying the rules correctly.

Regarding penalties, it is important to be clear about which penalties apply to which offence as they all have different penalty systems – late payment and late filing in particular, but also incorrect filing and failure to keep records. The chief assessor has commented in the past that it is very common for learners to give the penalties that apply to late filing in answer to a question about late payment and vice versa. This usually results in no marks being allocated to a question on this topic.

94   IRFAN

	True	False
An individual must retain their tax records for their business for 2016/17 until 5 April 2019		✓
If an individual is seven months late in submitting their tax return for 2016/17, they will receive a maximum penalty of £200		✓
The maximum penalty for a mistake in a tax return due to carelessness is 70%		✓
If an individual's balancing payment for 2016/17 is two months late they can be charged a penalty for late payment of 5%	✓	
A company with a period of account ending 30 September 2016 must submit its tax return by 30 September 2017	✓	
Interest is charged on late payments of balancing payments and instalments	✓	

Tutorial note

An individual's business records must be retained for 5 years after the filing date (i.e. 31 January following the end of the tax year). Therefore, the 2016/17 records must be kept until 31 January 2023.

The penalties for an individual filing a tax return late are as follows:

(i)   Within 3 months of the due date   =   £100 fixed penalty

(ii)   Between 3 to 6 months of the due date   =   Additional daily penalties of £10 per day

(Maximum 90 days)

(iii)   Between 6 to 12 months of due date   =   Additional 5% of tax due (Minimum £300)

(iv)   More than 12 months after the due date   =   Additional 5% of tax due (Minimum £300)

> *(v)   More than 12 months after the due date if the taxpayer withholds information:*
>
> *– deliberate and concealed = 100% (Minimum £300)*
>
> *– deliberate and not concealed = 70% (Minimum £300).*
>
> *The maximum penalty for incorrect returns depends on the behaviour of the taxpayer, and is calculated as a percentage of tax lost as follows:*
>
> *(i)   Careless mistake – no penalty*
>
> *(ii)   Failure to take reasonable care – 30%*
>
> *(iii)   Deliberate understatement – 70%*
>
> *(iv)   Deliberate understatement with concealment – 100%.*
>
> *In addition to tax and possible interest, late payment penalties are applied to unpaid tax. However, late payment penalties only apply to the final payment of income tax, class 2 and 4 NICs and capital gains tax.*
>
> *The amount due is:*
>
> *(i)   5% of the unpaid tax if it is more than one month late*
>
> *(ii)   A further 5% if more than six months late*
>
> *(iii)   A further 5% if more than 12 months late.*
>
> *A company must submit its tax return within 12 months of the end of the chargeable accounting period.*
>
> *Interest is payable on any tax paid late.*

95   COMPLIANCE CHECKS AND APPEALS

(a)   C

Tutorial note

HMRC must issue a written notice to initiate a compliance check and cannot issue a notice more than 12 months after the date the return was actually filed.

(b)   True or false

	True	False
A closed compliance check can be reopened within 9 months of the completion notice		✓
The taxpayer's right of appeal against an amended assessment on the closure of a compliance check must be made within 30 days of the completion notice	✓	
Where a company has submitted its tax return on time, the deadline for HMRC to commence a compliance check is two years after the end of the company's accounting period		✓

Tutorial note

A closed compliance check cannot be re-opened.

Appeals must be made within 30 days.

Where a company has submitted its tax return on time, the time limit for commencing a compliance check is one year after the actual filing date.

(c)   A

Tutorial note

An appeal can only be made on the basis of a point of law.

Note that the Supreme Court was previously known as the House of Lords.

96   NAGINA

	True	False
The maximum penalty for failing to keep records is £3,000 per accounting period	✓	
The maximum penalty for a failure to notify chargeability is 100% of the tax due but unpaid	✓	
A late payment penalty can apply to instalment payments of income tax		✓
Companies can choose whether to file paper tax returns or file online		✓

Tutorial note

The maximum penalty for notifying chargeability depends on the behaviour of the taxpayer, and is calculated in broadly the same way as the penalty for an incorrect return.

The late payment penalty only applies to the final payments of income tax and class 4 NICs and to the payment of class 2 NICs and capital gains tax, not instalment payments.

Companies must file their returns online.

97 PENALTIES

(a)   B

(b)   C

(c)   A

(d)   A

Tutorial note

Penalties for submitting a company's or an individual's tax return late are as follows:

(i)   Within 3 months of the due date   =   £100 fixed penalty

(ii)   Between 3 to 6 months of the due date   =   £200   fixed penalty

(iii)   Between 6 to 12 months of due date   =   Additional 10% of tax due

(iv)   More than 12 months after the due date   =   Additional 20% of tax due

The maximum penalty for incorrect returns depends on the behaviour of the taxpayer, and is calculated as a percentage of tax lost as follows:

(i)   Mistake – no penalty

(ii)   Failure to take reasonable care – 30%

(iii)   Deliberate understatement – 70%

(iv)   Deliberate understatement with concealment – 100%.

98 MANINDER

	True	False
The filing deadline for electronic submission of an individual's 2016/17 tax return is 31 January 2018	✓	
A self-employed individual is required to keep records to support his 2016/17 tax return until 31 January 2023	✓	
There is no penalty for late submission of an individual's tax return as long as it is less than 6 months late		✓
If a company makes a mistake in the tax return due to failure to take reasonable care, there is a penalty of 30%	✓	
An individual should make their first payment on account for 2016/17 on 31 January 2018		✓

Tutorial note

An individual can choose to file their return either on paper or electronically online:

(i)   If filing on paper, the due date is 31 October following the end of the tax year.

(ii)   Electronic filing must be submitted by 31 January following the end of the tax year.

An individual's business records must be retained for 5 years after the filing date (i.e. 31 January following the end of the tax year). Therefore, the 2016/17 records must be kept until 31 January 2023.

Penalties for submitting an individual's tax return late are as follows:

(i)   Within 3 months of the due date   =   £100 fixed penalty

(ii)   Between 3 to 6 months of the due date   =   Additional daily penalties of £10 per day

(Maximum 90 days)

(iii)   Between 6 to 12 months of due date   =   Additional 5% of tax due (Minimum £300)

(iv)   More than 12 months after the due date   =   Additional 5% of tax due (Minimum £300)

(v)   More than 12 months after the due date if the taxpayer withholds information:

– deliberate and concealed = 100% (Minimum £300)

– deliberate and not concealed = 70% (Minimum £300).

The maximum penalty for a company making a mistake on their return depends on the behaviour of the company, and is calculated as a percentage of tax lost as follows:

(i)   Mistake – no penalty

(ii)   Failure to take reasonable care – 30%

(iii)   Deliberate understatement – 70%

(iv)   Deliberate understatement with concealment – 100%.

A self-employed individual must pay 'Payments on account' for income tax and class 4 NICs based on the previous years' results on:

(i)   31 January in the tax year, and

(ii)   31 July following the end of the tax year.

99   JANET

	True	False
If an individual is eight months late in submitting their tax return for 2016/17, they will receive a penalty of £200		✓
The maximum penalties for errors made by individuals in their tax return vary from 20% to 100%		✓
If a company fails to keep records for the appropriate period of time, they can be fined up to £2,000		✓
A company with a period of account ending on 30 June 2016, must keep their records until 30 June 2024		✓
Late payment penalties are not normally imposed on payments on account	✓	

Tutorial note

Penalties for submitting an individual's tax return late are as follows:

(i)   Within 3 months of the due date = £100 fixed penalty

(ii)   Between 3 to 6 months of the due date =   Additional daily penalties of £10 per day

(Maximum 90 days)

(iii)   Between 6 to 12 months of due date = Additional 5% of tax due (Minimum £300)

(iv)   More than 12 months after the due date = Additional 5% of tax due (Minimum £300)

(v)   More than 12 months after the due date if the taxpayer withholds information:

– deliberate and concealed = 100% (Minimum £300)

– deliberate and not concealed = 70% (Minimum £300).

The maximum penalty for errors made by an individual in their tax return depends on the behaviour of the taxpayer, and is calculated as a percentage of tax lost as follows:

(i)   Mistake – no penalty

(ii)   Failure to take reasonable care – 30%

(iii)   Deliberate understatement – 70%

(iv)   Deliberate understatement with concealment – 100%.

Companies must keep records until six years from the end of the accounting period.

The maximum penalty for a company failing to keep records is £3,000 per accounting period affected.

Late payment penalties only apply to the final payment of income tax, class 2 and 4 NICs and capital gains tax, not instalment payments.

100 ETHICAL RULES (1)

Key answer tips

Make sure you read written questions like this very carefully.

In part (a) the question is asking you which statement is NOT correct; it is very easy to misread and ignore the not.

(a)   The answer is C.

The other three statements are correct.

Tutorial note

Whilst an accountant can be associated with returns that may omit information which would mislead HMRC, this is only true provided the information was not deliberately omitted and is more in the nature of supplementary information which would enhance understanding.

An accountant should not be associated with a return which has deliberately omitted sources of income or other information about taxable income.

(b)   The answer is C.

Tutorial note

The accountant can only share information with the client, unless the client gives authority for others to be informed.

101   ETHICAL RULES (2)

(a)   The answer is D.

The other three statements are correct.

Tutorial note

It is common practice for accountants to prepare tax returns for clients. However, the accountant can only prepare the return based on the information supplied by the client.

The client must always sign the return and the declaration included on the return, to confirm that they have supplied all relevant information.

It is the client's responsibility to submit a completed, signed form as his self-assessment of his own tax position.

(b)   The answer is C.

Tutorial note

An accountant generally needs the client's permission before revealing confidential information.

102 CLIENT ADVICE

(a)   The answer is C.

       The other three statements are correct.

Tutorial note

Tax evasion (such as deliberately failing to disclose all of your income) is illegal.

It is tax avoidance that uses legal means to reduce your tax bill.

(b)   The answer is C.

103 AAT STUDENT

(a)   The answer is B.

       The other three statements are correct.

Tutorial note

The duty of confidentiality to the client applies in all circumstances to all individuals, except where there is a legal, regulatory or professional duty to disclose (e.g. suspicion of money laundering).

An accountant cannot therefore disclose information to anyone without the client's permission, including the client's spouse or civil partner.

(b)   The answer is D.

Tutorial note

When money laundering is suspected an accountant should report his suspicions. This legal duty overrules the duty of confidentiality.

104 NASHEEN

	True	False
If a husband is ill, it is acceptable to discuss his tax affairs with his wife even if no letter of authorisation exists.		✓
Accountants must follow the rules of confidentiality irrespective of the situation.		✓

Tutorial note

The first statement is false because the duty of confidentiality to the client applies in all circumstances to all individuals, except where there is a legal, regulatory or professional duty to disclose (e.g. suspicion of money laundering).

An accountant cannot therefore disclose information to anyone without the client's permission, including the client's spouse or civil partner.

The second statement is false because when money laundering is suspected an accountant should report his suspicions. This legal duty overrules the duty of confidentiality.

105 TAX RETURN RESPONSIBILITY

The answer is C.

A taxpayer is ultimately responsible for ensuring that their tax return is accurately completed.

106 LAREDO

	True	False
All tax records for an individual should be kept for at least 4 years.		✓
The maximum penalty for not keeping records is £2,000.		✓
An individual whose income tax payable by self-assessment for the previous tax year is less than £1,000 is not required to make payments on account.	✓	
Tax on chargeable gains is paid in two instalments on 31 January in the tax year and 31 July following the end of the tax year.		✓

Tutorial note

Tax records should be kept for 1 year from 31 January following the tax year for personal records and 5 years for business records.

Taxpayers can be fined up to £3,000 for failure to keep records.

There are no instalments for capital gains tax.

The whole of the capital gains tax liability is due on 31 January following the end of the tax year (i.e. 31 January 2018 for the 2016/17 tax year).

WRITTEN QUESTIONS

Key answer tips

To answer a written question, you must make sure you have understood the scenario you are being asked about, and that your answer is specific to that situation and not just generalised facts. The chief assessor comments that often learners give very generic, basic answers that may be technically correct, but are not directly related to the scenario given.

107 MALIK

Dear Malik

Congratulations on the new contract. The new contract means that you will be required to pay both class 4 and class 2 national insurance contributions.

Class 2 national insurance contributions are currently at a fixed rate of £2.80 per week and therefore you would pay £2.80 x 52 = £145.60 per year, based on current figures.

Class 4 contributions are based on 9% of your taxable profits above the current limit of £8,060. Once you have estimated figures, I can provide more detailed calculations. If you are making payments on account of income tax, the class 4 contributions are paid in the same way. However, as your income tax liability was less than £1,000 for 2016/17, you do not have to make payments on account of income tax or national insurance for 2017/18. We will need to revisit this issue for 2018/19.

If you have any further queries please contact me.

AAT student

108 BAMBOO LTD

With regard to the understated rent, this appears to be a genuine mistake, rather than the financial controller not taking appropriate care. Your financial controller immediately informed HMRC of the issue. As a result, there should be no penalty.

The corporation tax return for Elm Ltd for the year ended 30 June 2015 was due by 30 June 2016. As the return was filed on 7 June 2016, it was not late and no penalty will be incurred.

If you have any further queries please contact me.

AAT student

Tutorial note

The maximum penalty for errors made in the tax return depends on the behaviour of the taxpayer, and is calculated as a percentage of tax lost as follows:

(i)   Mistake – no penalty

(ii)   Failure to take reasonable care – 30%

(iii)   Deliberate understatement – 70%

(iv)   Deliberate understatement with concealment – 100%.

109 SARA

Dear Sara

In response to your query, HMRC have the right to enquire into your 2015/16 tax return. They can start a compliance check within 12 months of the date that your return was filed, so they are within their powers, as you filed your return 6 months ago.

You should only send documents and written particulars to HMRC if they are requested as a part of the compliance check process.

At the end of the compliance check, a completion notice will be issued to you with details of the outcome. You have the right to appeal this notice within 30 days, via an informal review or a formal appeal to the Tax Tribunal, which is an independent body.

Please let me know if you need further assistance with this.

AAT student

Tutorial note

HMRC must issue a written notice to initiate a compliance check and cannot issue a notice more than 12 months after the date the return was actually filed.

110 CHARLIE

Dear Charlie,

Payments on account of your tax liability for any year must be paid by 31 January in that tax year, and by 31 July following the tax year. This is based on an estimate, using the preceding tax years' liability.

Therefore, when you made your tax payments on 31 January 2016 and 31 July 2016 for 2015/16, this was based on your liability for 2014/15.

When the final figures are sent to HMRC, if these two instalments are not enough to cover the full liability, a balancing payment is due on the 31 January following the tax year.

For 2016/17 your payments due will therefore be:

31 January 2017	(£8,600/2)	£4,300
31 July 2017	(£8,600/2)	£4,300
31 January 2018	(£9,000 – £8,600)	£400

I hope this makes things clearer. If you have any queries please do not hesitate to contact me.

Best regards

AAT Student

Tutorial note

A self-employed individual must pay 'Payments on account' for income tax and class 4 NICs based on the previous years' results on:

(i)   31 January in the tax year, and

(ii)   31 July following the end of the tax year.

111 MELANIE

Whether Melanie will be treated as carrying on a trade

An item of furniture could be a trading asset or an investment or for personal use so the 'subject matter' test is inconclusive.

The work carried out by Melanie in restoring the furniture would indicate that the furniture is a trading asset.

Melanie's motive in purchasing more furniture to renovate and sell is partly to make a profit, which is indicative of trading.

It is unlikely that the items of furniture **inherited** by Melanie will be regarded as trading assets. However, additional items of furniture **purchased** by Melanie for renovation and sale are likely to be regarded as trading assets.

Melanie is an investment banker. Restoring and selling furniture is not similar to any trading activity carried on by Melanie.

(Note: you were only required to explain Melanie's position in relation to four factors.)

112 CHARLOTTE

Charlotte,

Here is the information you requested. I hope it is helpful.

Tax payments

Income tax is paid by two instalments, the first on the 31 January in the tax year (31 January 2017 for 2016/17) and the second on the 31 July after the tax year (31 July 2017 for 2016/17).

These are based on half of your prior year income tax payable. No instalments are paid for capital gains tax.

Due on 31 January 2018

On 31 January 2018 you will have to pay the balance of any income tax due for 2016/17 and all of your 2016/17 capital gains tax. In your case this will be £6,230 which is your total liability of £14,230 less the £8,000 you have already paid by instalments.

In addition you will have to pay the first instalment of your 2017/18 income tax. This will be £4,665 as it is based on half of your 2016/17 income tax payable of £9,330.

This means that you must pay a total of £10,895 by 31 January 2018.

Consequences of late payment

If you pay tax late, then you are charged interest from the date you should have paid until the day the tax is actually paid.

In addition, if you make your balancing payment of £6,230 late you may be charged a late payment penalty. If the payment is more than 30 days late a penalty of 5% of the tax due can be charged which increases if the tax is paid more than 6 months late.

Kind regards

AAT student

Tutorial note

In addition to tax and possible interest, late payment penalties are applied to unpaid tax. However, late payment penalties only apply to the final payment of income tax, Class 4 NICs and capital gains tax.

The amount due is:

(i)   5% of the unpaid tax if it is more than 30 days late

(ii)   A further 5% if more than six months late

(iii)   A further 5% if more than 12 months late.

---

113 SOPHIA

There are several issues involved with not disclosing income to HMRC. Luckily this has not been going on for a long time so the consequences are not as bad as they could be.

1   Altering your 2015/16 tax return

Amendments to a tax return can be made by a taxpayer up to 12 months after the filing date. For a 2015/16 return the filing date is 31 January 2017. You can therefore make an amendment to your return to include the interest income and this should be done by 31 January 2018.

2   Penalty for incorrect return

As you have omitted some income from your tax return you have made an incorrect return. A penalty may be charged by HMRC and this varies according to whether they consider it to be a careless or deliberate error. A careless error can attract a penalty of up to 30% of the tax unpaid as a result of the error and a deliberate error a maximum penalty of 70% of unpaid tax.

The tax unpaid as a result of your error is £ 600 (40% of £1,500).

The penalties can be reduced if you disclose the income voluntarily before HMRC become aware of it. In your case it is likely that HMRC will treat this as a careless error and the maximum penalty they will charge is £180 (£600 × 30%) although this may be reduced to nil due to your disclosure.

3   Late payment penalty and interest

As well as a penalty for an incorrect return, interest will be due on the unpaid tax from the date it should have been paid (i.e. 31 January 2017).

A late payment penalty can also be charged. As the tax is between 6 and 12 months late this penalty could be 10% of the outstanding tax.

Best regards

AAT Student

Tutorial note

If the taxpayer files an incorrect tax return, a penalty equal to a percentage of the tax under declared may be charged. The penalty may be waived for inadvertent errors, as long as the taxpayer notifies HMRC of the error as soon as possible.

The percentage depends on the reason for the error.

Taxpayer behaviour	Maximum penalty (% of tax lost)
Mistake	No penalty
Failure to take reasonable care	30%
Deliberate understatement	70%
Deliberate understatement with concealment	100%

The penalties may be reduced at HMRC discretion, depending on the type of penalty and whether the taxpayer makes an unprompted disclosure of the error.

TAX RETURNS

Key answer tips

The chief assessor has highlighted the most common errors made by learners in this task in the past.

The corporation tax return is one in which learners tend to perform really well and clearly take their time ensuring that sub-totals are also completed.

In the self-employed return there are two main errors made by learners. One is to forget to adjust for the depreciation shown in the first column. The same figure should always appear in both box 29 and 44. Also, some learners simply list the disallowed figures in the first boxes in the second (disallowable expenses) column, in any order. So if there are five adjustments to be made, boxes 32 to 36 would be completed. It is important to note the narrative for each box and to include the disallowable items in the appropriate box to match the equivalent expense entry in the left hand column.

114   HUMMEL LTD

Tax calculation

Turnover

145	Total turnover from trade	£	**1 0 0 0 0 0 0** · 0 0

| 150 | Banks, building societies, insurance companies and other financial concerns – put an 'X' in this box if you do not have a recognised turnover and have not made an entry in box 145 | |

Income

155	Trading profits	£	**5 8 5 0 0 0** · 0 0
160	Trading losses brought forward claimed against profits	£	**4 7 0 0 0** · 0 0
165	Net trading profits – *box 155 minus box 160*	£	**5 3 8 0 0 0** · 0 0
170	Bank, building society or other interest, and profits from non-trading loan relationships	£	**2 0 0 0 0** · 0 0

| 172 | Put an 'X' in box 172 if the figure in box 170 is net of carrying back a deficit from a later accounting period | |

175	Annual payments not otherwise charged to Corporation Tax and from which Income Tax has not been deducted	£	· 0 0
180	Non-exempt dividends or distributions from non-UK resident companies	£	· 0 0
185	Income from which Income Tax has been deducted	£	· 0 0
190	Income from a property business	£	**2 0 0 0 0 0** · 0 0
195	Non-trading gains on intangible fixed assets	£	· 0 0
200	Tonnage Tax profits	£	· 0 0
205	Income not falling under any other heading	£	· 0 0

Chargeable gains

210	Gross chargeable gains	£	**1 1 0 0 0 0** · 0 0
215	Allowable losses including losses brought forward	£	**4 9 0 0** · 0 0
220	Net chargeable gains – *box 210 minus box 215*	£	**1 0 5 1 0 0** · 0 0

Profits before deductions and reliefs

225	Losses brought forward against certain investment income	£	· 0 0
230	Non-trade deficits on loan relationships (including interest) and derivative contracts (financial instruments) brought forward	£	· 0 0
235	Profits before other deductions and reliefs – *net sum of boxes 165 to 205 and 220 minus sum of boxes 225 and 230*	£	**8 6 3 1 0 0** · 0 0

115 ROYLE LTD

Tax calculation
Turnover

145 Total turnover from trade £ 2900000 . 0 0

150 Banks, building societies, insurance companies and other financial concerns –
put an 'X' in this box if you do not have a recognised turnover and have not made an entry in box 145

Income

155 Trading profits £ 350000 . 0 0

160 Trading losses brought forward claimed against profits £ . 0 0

165 Net trading profits – *box 155 minus box 160* £ 350000 . 0 0

170 Bank, building society or other interest, and profits from non-trading loan relationships £ 6000 . 0 0

172 Put an 'X' in box 172 if the figure in box 170 is net of carrying back a deficit from a later accounting period

175 Annual payments not otherwise charged to Corporation Tax and from which Income Tax has not been deducted £ . 0 0

180 Non-exempt dividends or distributions from non–UK resident companies £ . 0 0

185 Income from which Income Tax has been deducted £ . 0 0

190 Income from a property business £ 20000 . 0 0

195 Non-trading gains on intangible fixed assets £ . 0 0

200 Tonnage Tax profits £ . 0 0

205 Income not falling under any other heading £ . 0 0

Chargeable gains

210 Gross chargeable gains £ 18000 . 0 0

215 Allowable losses including losses brought forward £ 3800 . 0 0

220 Net chargeable gains – *box 210 minus box 215* £ 14200 . 0 0

Profits before deductions and reliefs

225 Losses brought forward against certain investment income £ . 0 0

230 Non-trade deficits on loan relationships (including interest) and derivative contracts (financial instruments) brought forward £ . 0 0

235 Profits before other deductions and reliefs – *net sum of boxes 165 to 205 and 220 minus sum of boxes 225 and 230* £ 390200 . 0 0

116 JORDAN

Business expenses

Please read the 'Self-employment (full) notes' before filling in this section.

Total expenses	Disallowable expenses
If your annual turnover was below £83,000, you may just put your total expenses in box 31	Use this column if the figures in boxes 17 to 30 include disallowable amounts
17 Cost of goods bought for resale or goods used £ 2 0 8 1 7 8 · 0 0	**32** £ · 0 0
18 Construction industry – payments to subcontractors £ · 0 0	**33** £ · 0 0
19 Wages, salaries and other staff costs £ 3 5 6 0 4 · 0 0	**34** £ 1 8 0 0 0 · 0 0
20 Car, van and travel expenses £ 1 3 1 1 2 · 0 0	**35** £ 2 6 9 0 · 0 0
21 Rent, rates, power and insurance costs £ 1 4 2 4 0 · 0 0	**36** £ 3 0 0 0 · 0 0
22 Repairs and renewals of property and equipment £ 3 4 0 · 0 0	**37** £ · 0 0
23 Phone, fax, stationery and other office costs £ 7 4 2 · 0 0	**38** £ · 0 0
24 Advertising and business entertainment costs £ · 0 0	**39** £ · 0 0
25 Interest on bank and other loans £ · 0 0	**40** £ · 0 0
26 Bank, credit card and other financial charges £ · 0 0	**41** £ · 0 0
27 Irrecoverable debts written off £ 1 5 4 0 · 0 0	**42** £ 2 6 8 · 0 0
28 Accountancy, legal and other professional fees £ 9 8 0 · 0 0	**43** £ · 0 0
29 Depreciation and loss/profit on sale of assets £ 6 1 4 4 · 0 0	**44** £ 6 1 4 4 · 0 0
30 Other business expenses £ 1 7 7 8 · 0 0	**45** £ 2 8 0 · 0 0
31 Total expenses (total of boxes 17 to 30) £ 2 8 2 6 5 8 · 0 0	**46** Total disallowable expenses (total of boxes 32 to 45) £ 3 0 3 8 2 · 0 0

SA103F 2016   Page SEF 2

117 MR BODDERS

Business expenses

Please read the 'Self-employment (full) notes' before filling in this section.

Total expenses	Disallowable expenses
If your annual turnover was below £83,000, you may just put your total expenses in box 31	Use this column if the figures in boxes 17 to 30 include disallowable amounts

17 Cost of goods bought for resale or goods used
£ 1 0 8 1 9 5 . 0 0

32
£ . 0 0

18 Construction industry – payments to subcontractors
£ . 0 0

33
£ . 0 0

19 Wages, salaries and other staff costs
£ 6 5 6 5 0 . 0 0

34
£ 3 0 0 0 . 0 0

20 Car, van and travel expenses
£ 1 0 1 1 0 . 0 0

35
£ 1 4 4 0 . 0 0

21 Rent, rates, power and insurance costs
£ 1 2 2 5 0 . 0 0

36
£ 4 0 0 0 . 0 0

22 Repairs and renewals of property and equipment
£ . 0 0

37
£ . 0 0

23 Phone, fax, stationery and other office costs
£ 2 7 5 5 . 0 0

38
£ . 0 0

24 Advertising and business entertainment costs
£ 8 6 6 5 . 0 0

39
£ 2 3 1 0 . 0 0

25 Interest on bank and other loans
£ . 0 0

40
£ . 0 0

26 Bank, credit card and other financial charges
£ . 0 0

41
£ . 0 0

27 Irrecoverable debts written off
£ 5 1 0 . 0 0

42
£ . 0 0

28 Accountancy, legal and other professional fees
£ 2 9 8 0 . 0 0

43
£ . 0 0

29 Depreciation and loss/profit on sale of assets
£ 1 6 1 4 0 . 0 0

44
£ 1 6 1 4 0 . 0 0

30 Other business expenses
£ 1 7 6 0 . 0 0

45
£ . 0 0

31 Total expenses (total of boxes 17 to 30)
£ 2 2 9 0 1 5 . 0 0

46 Total disallowable expenses (total of boxes 32 to 45)
£ 2 6 8 9 0 . 0 0

SA103F 2016   Page SEF 2

118   LYNNE AND SHIRLEY PETERS

PARTNERSHIP STATEMENT (SHORT) for the year ended 5 April 2017

Please read these instructions before completing the Statement

Use these pages to allocate partnership income if the only income for the relevant return period was trading and professional income or taxed interest and alternative finance receipts from banks and building societies. Otherwise you must download or ask the SA Orderline for the 'Partnership Statement (Full)' pages to record details of the allocation of all the partnership income. Go to **www.gov.uk/self-assessment-forms-and-helpsheets**

Step 1   Fill in boxes 1 to 29 and boxes A and B as appropriate. Get the figures you need from the relevant boxes in the Partnership Tax Return. Complete a separate Statement for each accounting period covered by this Partnership Tax Return and for each trade or profession carried on by the partnership.

Step 2   Then allocate the amounts in boxes 11 to 29 attributable to each partner using the allocation columns on this page and page 7, read the Partnership Tax Return Guide, go to www.gov.uk/self-assessment-forms-and-helpsheets
If the partnership has more than 3 partners, please photocopy page 7.

Step 3   Each partner will need a copy of their allocation of income to fill in their personal tax return.

PARTNERSHIP INFORMATION
If the partnership business includes a trade or profession, enter here the accounting period for which appropriate items in this statement are returned.

Start	**1**	01 / 04 / 16
End	**2**	31 / 03 / 17
Nature of trade	**3**	Event organisers

MIXED PARTNERSHIPS

Tick here if this Statement is drawn up using Corporation Tax rules **4**

Tick here if this Statement is drawn up using tax rules for non-residents **5**

Individual partner details

6 Name of partner   Lynne Peters

Address

Postcode

Date appointed as a partner (if during 2015–16 or 2016–17)

7 / /

Partner's Unique Taxpayer Reference (UTR)

8

Date ceased to be a partner (if during 2015–16 or 2016–17)

9 / /

Partner's National Insurance number

10

Partnership's profits, losses, income, tax credits, etc

Partner's share of profits, losses, income, tax credits, etc

Copy figures in boxes 11 to 29 to boxes in the individual's **Partnership (short)** pages as shown below

Tick this box if the items entered in the box had foreign tax taken off ▼

• for an accounting period ended in 2016–17						
from box 3.83 Profit from a trade or profession	**A**	**11** £ 230,400	Profit	**11** £ 138,240	Copy this figure to box 8
from box 3.82 Adjustment on change of basis		**11A** £		**11A** £	Copy this figure to box 10
from box 3.84 Loss from a trade or profession	**B**	**12** £	Loss	**12** £	Copy this figure to box 8
from box 10.4 Business Premises Renovation Allowance		**12A** £		**12A** £	Copy this figure to box 15
• for the period 6 April 2016 to 5 April 2017*						
from box 7.9A UK taxed interest and taxed alternative finance receipts		**22** £ 6,210		**22** £ 3,726	Copy this figure to box 28
from box 3.97 CIS deductions made by contractors on account of tax		**24** £ 2,800		**24** £ 1,680	Copy this figure to box 30
from box 3.98 Other tax taken off trading income		**24A** £		**24A** £	Copy this figure to box 31
from box 7.8A Income Tax taken off		**25** £		**25** £	Copy this figure to box 29
from box 3.117 Partnership charges		**29** £ 4,000		**29** £ 2,400	Copy this figure to box 4, 'Other tax reliefs' section on page Ai 2 in your personal tax return

* if you are a 'CT Partnership' see the Partnership Tax Return Guide

SA800 2016   PARTNERSHIP TAX RETURN: PAGE 6

Section 3

MOCK ASSESSMENT QUESTIONS

TASK 1 **(12 marks)**

Safari Ltd, a UK company, has the following statement of profit or loss for the year ended 30 June 2016:

	£	£
Revenue		350,569
Less: Cost of sales		(195,053)
Gross profit		155,516
Other income		10,000
Wages and salaries	29,009	
Rent and rates	10,272	
Loss on the sale of a machine	400	
Repairs and maintenance	3,516	
Travelling and entertaining	2,357	
Motor expenses	2,814	
Legal and professional fees	4,123	
Irrecoverable debts	(756)	
Depreciation	3,656	
Other general expenses	1,225	
		(56,616)
Net profit		108,900

The following further information is given:

(1) **Other income**

This comprises bank deposit interest of £7,000 for the year received on 30 June 2016, and rent receivable of £3,000 for the year ended 30 June 2016.

(2) **Repairs and maintenance**

Included in this item is £1,740 incurred for replacing an obsolete machine with a new state-of-the-art version and £300 for the redecoration of a new office.

(3) **Travelling and entertaining expenses**

These include expenses of entertaining UK customers of £391 and gifts to customers of bottles of champagne costing £634 (cost approximately £45 each).

(4)   **Legal and professional fees**

The figure in the accounts is made up as follows:

	£
Legal fees in connection with new office purchase	390
Legal fees in connection with action by customer regarding faulty goods	996
Payment to customer for breach of contract	1,440
Accountancy charges	1,297

(5)   **Irrecoverable debts**

The figure in the accounts is made up as follows:

	£
Trade debt recoveries	(278)
Decrease in provision for irrecoverable debts	(478)
	(756)

(6)   **Other general expenses**

These include a donation of £240 to the Labour Party, and a donation of £30 to the NSPCC (a national charity).

Use the grid below to calculate the adjusted trading profit of the year for tax purposes. Where you wish to deduct a figure put it in brackets. If an item needs no adjustment include a zero '0'.

	£
Net profit	108,900
Bank deposit interest	
Rent receivable	
Wages and salaries	
Rent and rates	
Loss on the sale of a machine	
Replacing obsolete machine	
Redecoration of new office	
Entertaining UK customers	
Gifts to customers	
Motor expenses	
Legal fees in connection with new office purchase	
Legal fees in connection with action by customer regarding faulty goods	
Payment to customer for breach of contract	
Accountancy charges	
Trade debt recoveries	
Decrease in provision for irrecoverable debts	
Depreciation	
Labour Party donation	
NSPCC donation	
Tax adjusted trading profit	

TASK 2 (14 marks)

Scharrett Ltd has the following non-current asset information for the seven month period ended 31 July 2016:

	£
Balances brought forward as at 1 January 2016:	
General pool	14,000
Special rate pool	16,000
Additions in January 2016:	
Machinery	282,250
Finance Director's Car (Nissan) (40% private use)	15,000
Managing Director's Car (Audi) (75% private use)	32,000
Disposals in February 2016:	
Machinery (Cost £11,000)	10,100
Managing Director's car (Renault) (Cost £17,200)	13,600

The cars have CO_2 emissions as follows:

Nissan	70 g/km
Audi	126 g/km
Renault	185 g/km

Use the grid below to calculate Scharret Ltd's total capital allowances and show the balances to carry forward to the next accounting period.

TASK 3 (12 marks)

(a) Freddy started trading on 1 January 2013. He prepares his first set of accounts to 31 May 2014 and then to 31 May each year.

The adjusted profits were as follows:

	£
Period ended 31 May 2014	19,040
Year ended 31 May 2015	43,200
Year ended 31 May 2016	48,000

(i) In which tax year did Freddy start trading?

A 2011/12

B 2012/13

C 2013/14

D 2014/15

(ii) What are Freddy's taxable trading profits for the first tax year of trading?

A £19,040

B £4,760

C £4,480

D £3,360

(iii) What are Freddy's taxable trading profits for the second tax year of trading?

A £43,200

B £19,040

C £13,440

D £12,693

(iv) What are Freddy's taxable trading profits for the third tax year of trading?

A £13,440

B £19,040

C £38,240

D £43,200

(v) What are Freddy's taxable trading profits for the fourth tax year of trading?

A £13,440

B £43,200

C £47,200

D £48,000

(vi) What are Freddy's overlap profits? £ ☐

(b)   Gavin and Stacey are in partnership, and have always shared profits in the ratio 60%:40%.

It was then decided that from 1 June 2016 Gavin would be awarded a salary of £24,000 per annum to recognise the extra work that he had taken on. The remainder of the profits continue to be shared in the ratio 60%:40%.

For the year ended 31 January 2017, the tax adjusted trading profits were £180,000.

Calculate the 2016/17 assessment for each partner.

Gavin	£
Stacey	£

TASK 4   **(12 marks)**

(a)   Mark the following statements as true or false

	True	False
If a company pays interest on a loan to buy a new factory, the interest is deducted from non-trade interest income in the corporation tax computation.		
Legal costs incurred in writing off an irrecoverable debt due from a customer may be deducted from non-trade interest income in the corporation tax computation.		
Augmented profits includes all dividends received during the accounting period.		
Small donations to local charities must be disallowed in arriving at trading profits and relieved as qualifying charitable donations.		
The accrued amount of qualifying charitable donations is deducted from total profits to arrive at taxable total profits.		
If Ennis Ltd (an SME) spends £80,000 on qualifying research and development it can deduct a total of £184,000 in arriving at its adjusted trading profit.		

(b)   Walkden Ltd has previously prepared accounts to 31 December. In 2016 the company changes its year end and prepares accounts from 1 January 2016 to 31 May 2017.

The adjusted trading profit for the period before deducting capital allowances is £690,540.

At 1 January 2016 there was a balance in the general pool of £90,000. Plant and machinery costing £185,000 was purchased on 1 September 2016.

Complete the following grid:

	First period	Second period
Period ends on: (Insert date)		
Length of period (Insert number of months)		
Adjusted trade profits before CAs	£	£
Capital allowances	£	£
Adjusted trade profit after CAs	£	£

(c)   Due dates

   (i)   What is the deadline for the payment of corporation tax for a single company with the year end 31 August 2016 that has augmented profits below £1,500,000?

   [   ]

   (ii)   By when must a company with the year ended 31 May 2016 submit its corporation tax return?

   [   ]

   (iii)   What is the last instalment payment date for a large company with a 31 March 2017 year end?

   [   ]

TASK 5   (4 marks)

(a)   Matthew's sole trader business has made an accounting profit of £5,000 for 2016/17. His tax adjusted trading profit was £6,100

   The total amount of NICs payable by Matthew is: £ [   ]

(b)   Clive has taxable trading profits of £53,000 for 2016/17.

   The total amount of class 4 NICs payable by Clive is: £ [   ]

(c)   Jackie's business has made a taxable trading profit of £80,000 for 2016/17.

   The amount of class 2 NICs payable by Jackie for the year is: £ [   ]

TASK 6 (6 marks)

(a) For each of the following types of loss for a company, tick which income it can be set against in the **current year**:

Note that if a loss can be set against total profits you should only tick that column.

	Trading profits	Chargeable gains	Property income	Total profits before QCDs	No loss relief available
Trading loss					
Capital loss					

(b) For each of the following types of loss for a company, tick which income it can be set against in the **prior year**:

Note that if a loss can be set against total profits you should only tick that column.

	Trading profits	Chargeable gains	Property income	Total profits before QCDs	No loss relief available
Trading loss					
Capital loss					

(c) For each of the following types of loss for a company, tick which income it can be set against in the **following year**:

Note that if a loss can be set against total profits you should only tick that column.

	Trading profits	Chargeable gains	Property income	Total profits before QCDs	No loss relief available
Trading loss					
Capital loss					

TASK 7 (10 marks)

(a) You recently received the following email from Liam, a self-employed individual, who is one of your clients.

> Due to a recent flood at our premises, we are moving to a small temporary office next week. My accounts assistant, Jenny, has recommended that, for the sake of confidentiality, I shred all of the business tax records that relate to 2014/15 (the tax year in which I started my business) as I have not had any queries regarding my income tax returns and all are finalised. Obviously I'll keep my personal records at home. I presume that is OK.
>
> Jenny has also recommended that I delay my next income tax balancing payment for 2 months, just to help with cash flow following the flood. I presume that is acceptable?
>
> Can you reply to me about these two issues, please?

Prepare an appropriate response to Liam.

(b)   Dominic asks whether the following statements are true or false.

Tick the appropriate box for each statement.

	True	False
The maximum penalty for mistakes in a tax return due to carelessness is 50%		
A company with a period of account ending 30 September 2016 must pay a penalty of £3,000 if it does not retain its records until 30 September 2022		
Interest is charged on late payment of balancing payments only, not payments on account		
If an individual's balancing payment for 2016/17 is two months late they can be charged a late payment penalty of 5%		
If an individual is eight months late in submitting their tax return for 2016/17, they will receive a penalty of £200		
Only AAT members, not students, are governed by the AAT ethical code		
There are no circumstances in which client confidentiality can be breached		

TASK 8   (6 marks)

Complete the return below as far as is possible, using the following information.

In the year ended 30 September 2016 Hammer Ltd had made sales of £920,000 leading to a taxable trading profit of £538,200.

The company also had rental profits of £185,000, interest income of £18,400, chargeable gains of £101,000.

Hammer Ltd had trading losses brought forward of £72,000.

Tax calculation
Turnover

145	Total turnover from trade	£		• 0 0

150	Banks, building societies, insurance companies and other financial concerns – put an 'X' in this box if you do not have a recognised turnover and have not made an entry in box 145	☐

Income

155	Trading profits	£	• 0 0

160	Trading losses brought forward claimed against profits	£	• 0 0

165	Net trading profits – *box 155 minus box 160*	£	• 0 0

170	Bank, building society or other interest, and profits from non-trading loan relationships	£	• 0 0

172	Put an 'X' in box 172 if the figure in box 170 is net of carrying back a deficit from a later accounting period	☐

175	Annual payments not otherwise charged to Corporation Tax and from which Income Tax has not been deducted	£	• 0 0

Income *continued*

180	Non-exempt dividends or distributions from non–UK resident companies	£	• 0 0

185	Income from which Income Tax has been deducted	£	• 0 0

190	Income from a property business	£	• 0 0

195	Non-trading gains on intangible fixed assets	£	• 0 0

200	Tonnage Tax profits	£	• 0 0

205	Income not falling under any other heading	£	• 0 0

Chargeable gains

210	Gross chargeable gains	£	• 0 0

215	Allowable losses including losses brought forward	£	• 0 0

220	Net chargeable gains – *box 210 minus box 215*	£	• 0 0

Profits before deductions and reliefs

225	Losses brought forward against certain investment income	£	• 0 0

230	Non-trade deficits on loan relationships (including interest) and derivative contracts (financial instruments) brought forward	£	• 0 0

235	Profits before other deductions and reliefs – *net sum of boxes 165 to 205 and 220 minus sum of boxes 225 and 230*	£	• 0 0

TASK 9 (8 marks)

(a) Lena disposed of five assets in 2016/17.

Tick the appropriate box to indicate which disposals are chargeable assets and which are exempt assets for capital gains tax purposes.

	Chargeable asset	Exempt asset
Antique sideboard – sold for £23,000 to an auction house		
Vintage classic car – Morris Minor worth £55,000 – gifted to daughter		
Unquoted shares in Febroy Ltd – sold for less than they were bought for		
Treasury stock quoted on the UK stock exchange – sold on the open market for considerably more than it was bought for		
Holiday home in Wales – sold at a profit to neighbours. Lena lives in her main residence in Birmingham		

(b) Pelican Ltd sold an antique vase for £8,450 in August 2016.

It was purchased in April 2009 for £3,180.

The relevant indexation factor is 0.244.

Which of the following is the correct chargeable gain?

A £4,494

B £5,270

C £Nil – it is an exempt asset

D £4,083

(c) Vincent Ltd owns 20 acres of land, which it bought in May 2000 for £168,000.

In August 2016, Vincent Ltd sold 8 acres for £235,000, when the remaining 12 acres had a market value of £320,000.

The indexation factor from May 2000 to August 2016 was 0.541.

Complete the following computation:

	£
Sale proceeds	
Cost	
Indexation allowance	
Chargeable gain	

TASK 10 (10 marks)

J plc bought 1,500 shares in Leanne Ltd for £14,500 on 15 July 2010.

A bonus issue of 1 for 6 shares was made on 7 May 2011.

On 31 October 2016 the company bought 400 shares for £15.50 per share.

On 5 November 2016, the company sold 750 shares for £16.80 per share.

Indexation factors were:

July 2010 to May 2011	0.052
May 2011 to November 2016	0.124
July 2010 to November 2016	0.182
October 2016 to November 2016	0.002

Calculate the chargeable gain on the disposal of these shares.

TASK 11 (6 marks)

(a)   A factory was sold by Olivia for £950,000 in October 2016 realising a gain of £370,000.

Which of the following statements is correct in relation to rollover relief?

A   If Olivia purchases a replacement factory for £900,000 in June 2017 then she can use rollover relief to defer £320,000 of the gain

B   If Olivia purchases a replacement factory for £980,000 in November 2019 then she can use rollover relief to defer all the gain

C   If Olivia purchases some shares in an unquoted trading company for £980,000 in February 2017 then she can claim rollover relief

D   If Olivia reinvests in a qualifying asset within the qualifying time period then the gain of £370,000 is automatically deferred

(b)   Elvis has disposed of several capital assets in 2016/17 and realised the following gains and losses:

	Disposal to:	£
Chargeable gain	Aunt	23,000
Chargeable gain	Unconnected person	14,500
Allowable loss	Brother	(3,000)
Allowable loss	Friend	(2,600)

Elvis has unutilised capital losses relating to 2015/16 of £5,600.

(i)   What is Elvis's taxable gain for 2016/17?   £

(ii)   What is the capital loss remaining to carry forward to 2017/18?   £

(c)   Tony has taxable income of £30,215 for 2016/17. He has made a gain on the disposal of a painting of £26,000.

(i)   What is Tony's capital gains tax liability for 2016/17?   £

(ii)   What is the due date of payment?

Section 4

MOCK ASSESSMENT ANSWERS

TASK 1

Safari Ltd – Adjusted trading profit – year ended 30 June 2016

	£
Net profit	108,900
Bank deposit interest	(7,000)
Rent receivable	(3,000)
Wages and salaries	0
Rent and rates	0
Loss on the sale of a machine	400
Replacing obsolete machine	1,740
Redecoration of new office	0
Entertaining UK customers	391
Gifts to customers	634
Motor expenses	0
Legal fees in connection with new office purchase	390
Legal fees in connection with action by customer regarding faulty goods	0
Payment to customer for breach of contract	0
Accountancy charges	0
Trade debt recoveries	0
Decrease in provision for irrecoverable debts	0
Depreciation	3,656
Labour Party donation	240
NSPCC donation	30
Tax adjusted trading profit	106,381

Tutorial note

1 *Depreciation, the loss on the sale of the machine, the cost of the new machine and legal fees in relation to the new office are all capital in nature and must be added back.*

2 *The £300 redecoration costs in respect of the new office are considered to be allowable, following the decision in the Odeon Theatres case.*

3 *Entertaining is not an allowable deduction, unless it is in respect of entertaining staff.*

> 4   *Gifts to customers costing less than £50 per person per year and carrying a conspicuous advertisement for the business are tax allowable, unless they are gifts of food, drink or tobacco. Although the bottles of champagne cost less than £50 each, the cost is disallowed as the gift is of drink.*
>
> 5   *Legal fees and payment in connection with faulty goods are allowable, as they are trade related costs.*
>
> 6   *Donations to political parties are not allowable deductions.*
>
> 7   *Donations to a national charity are not allowable trading expenses, regardless of size.*
>
> 8   *Such donations made by a company are allowable for tax, but not as a deduction in the adjustment of profits computation. They must therefore be added back and relief is given as a deduction from total profits in the TTP computation.*

TASK 2

Scharrett Ltd – Capital allowances computation – seven months ended 31 July 2016

	£	General pool £	Special rate pool £	Total £
TWDV b/f		14,000	16,000	
Additions – No AIA				
Managing director's car (Audi)		32,000		
Additions – With AIA				
Machinery	282,250			
Less: AIA (W)	(116,667)			116,667
		165,583		
Disposals (Lower of Cost and SP)		(10,100)	(13,600)	
		201,483	2,400	
Less: WDA				
(18% × 7/12)		(21,156)		21,156
(8% × 7/12)			(112)	112
Addition – 100% FYA				
Low emission car (Nissan)	15,000			
Less: FYA (100%)	(15,000)			15,000
		Nil		
TWDV c/f		180,327	2,288	
Total allowances				152,935

Working: The maximum AIA for the seven months ended 31 July 2016 is £116,667 (£200,000 × 7/12).

Tutorial note

1   Private use of assets by an employee is irrelevant in a capital allowances computation; the allowances are available in full. The individual is assessed on the private use element in their personal income tax computation as an employment benefit.

2   Capital allowances on car purchases are calculated based on the CO_2 emissions of the car as follows:

–   new car with CO_2 emissions of ≤ 75 g/km:
eligible for a FYA of 100% (i.e. the Nissan)

– CO_2 emissions of between 76 – 130 g/km:
put in main pool and eligible for a WDA at 18% (i.e. the Audi)

– CO_2 emissions of > 130 g/km:
put in special rate pool and eligible for a WDA at 8% (i.e. the Renault)

3   Disposals are deducted at the lower of cost and sale proceeds. The deduction for the machinery is therefore £10,100.

4   The accounting period is seven months in length, therefore the AIA and the WDA must be time apportioned by 7/12. However, the FYA is never time apportioned.

TASK 3

Freddy

(a)   (i)   B

(ii)   D

(iii)   C

(iv)   A

(v)   B

(vi)   £11,200

Working

Tax year	Basis period		Assessment £
2012/13	Actual basis		
	1 January 2013 – 5 April 2013	(3/17 × £19,040)	3,360
2013/14	Actual basis		
	6 April 2013 – 5 April 2014	(12/17 × £19,040)	13,440
2014/15	12 month ending 31 May 2014		
	1 June 2013 – 31 May 2014	(12/17 × £19,040)	13,440
2015/16	Current year basis		
	year ended 31 May 2015		43,200
Overlap profits	1 June 2013 – 5 April 2014	(10/17 × £19,040)	11,200

(b)　**Allocation of profits**

	Total £	Gavin £	Stacey £
Period to: 31 May 2016 (£180,000 × 4/12)	60,000		
Allocate (60%:40%)		36,000	24,000
Period to: 31 January 2017 (£180,000 × 8/12)	120,000		
Salary (£24,000 × 8/12)	(16,000)	16,000	
Balance allocated (60%:40%)	104,000	62,400	41,600
	180,000	114,400	65,600

TASK 4

Walkden Ltd

(a)　Mark the following statements as true or false

	True	False
If a company pays interest on a loan to buy a new factory, the interest is deducted from non-trade interest income in the corporation tax computation.		✓
Legal costs incurred in writing off an irrecoverable debt due from a customer may be deducted from non-trade interest income in the corporation tax computation.		✓
Augmented profits includes all dividends received during the accounting period.		✓
Small donations to local charities must be disallowed in arriving at trading profits and relieved as qualifying charitable donations.		✓
The accrued amount of qualifying charitable donations is deducted from total profits to arrive at taxable total profits.		✓
If Ennis Ltd (an SME), spends £80,000 on qualifying research and development it can deduct a total of £184,000 in arriving at its adjusted trading profit.	✓	

Tutorial note

1   *Interest on a loan to buy a new factory is trade interest and can be deducted from trade profits.*

2   *Costs of writing off an irrecoverable debt due from a customer relate to a trade debt and are normal trading expenses. The cost of writing off a **loan** to a customer would be a non-trade item, but that is not the case here.*

3   *Augmented profits excludes dividends from 51% group companies.*

4   *Small donations to local charities are allowed as trade expenses not as QCDs.*

5   *QCDs are allowed on a paid basis not an accrued basis.*

6   *Companies which are small or medium sized enterprises (SMEs), can deduct a total of 230% of the cost of qualifying research and development from their profits.*

If Ennis Ltd spends £80,000 they can deduct a total of £184,000 (£80,000 × 230%) in arriving at their adjusted trade profits.

(b)

	First period	**Second period**
Period ends on: (Insert date)	31 December 2016	31 May 2017
Length of period (Insert number of months)	12	5
Adjusted trade profits before CAs	£487,440	£203,100
Capital allowances	£201,200	£5,535
Adjusted trade profit after CAs	£286,240	£197,565

Workings

(1)   Adjusted trade profits before CAs

	£	£
Adjusted trade profits split 12/17 : 5/17	187,440	203,100

(2) Walkden Ltd – Capital allowances computation

	£	General pool £	Total allowances £
12 months to 31 December 2016			
Balance b/f		90,000	
Addition qualifying for AIA	185,000		
Less: AIA	(185,000)		185,000
		Nil	
WDA (£90,000 × 18%)		(16,200)	16,200
Tax WDV c/f		73,800	
Total allowances			201,200
5 months to 31 May 2017			
WDA (£73,800 × 18% × 5/12)		(5,535)	5,535
Tax WDV c/f		68,265	
			5,535

Tutorial note

When a company prepares accounts for a period exceeding 12 months it will have two accounting periods, the first for 12 months and the second for the balance of the period.

The adjusted trading profit before capital allowances must be time apportioned into the two periods.

Two separate capital allowances computations must be prepared, one for each period. The second period will be less than 12 months so any AIA or WDA must be time apportioned.

(c) **Due dates**

(i) 1 June 2017
(i.e. 9 months and one day after the end of the chargeable accounting period)

(ii) 31 May 2017
(i.e. 12 months after the end of the financial accounting period)

(iii) 14 July 2017
(i.e. 14th day of the 16th month after the start of the chargeable accounting period)

TASK 5

Matthew, Clive and Jackie

(a)   £145.60. Class 2 NICs are due where taxable trading profits exceed £5,965.

(b)   Class 4 NICs

	£ p
(£43,000 – £8,060) = £34,325 × 9%	3,144.60
(£53,000 – £43,000) = £10,000 × 2%	200.00
	3,344.60

(c)   Class 2 NICs

	£ p
(£2.80 × 52 weeks)	145.60

Tutorial note

Self-employed taxpayers pay class 4 NICs based on their taxable trading profits in excess of £8,060 and the fixed rate class 2 NICs of £2.80 per week provided taxable trading profits exceed £5,965.

TASK 6

Losses

(a)   Income the company can set its loss against in the **current year**

	Trading profits	Chargeable gains	Property income	Total profits before QCDs	No loss relief available
Trading loss				✓	
Capital loss		✓			

(b)   Income the company can set its loss against in the **previous year**

	Trading profits	Chargeable gains	Property income	Total profits before QCDs	No loss relief available
Trading loss				✓	
Capital loss					✓

(c) Income the company can set its loss against in the **following year**

	Trading profits	Chargeable gains	Property income	Total profits before QCDs	No loss relief available
Trading loss	✓				
Capital loss		✓			

TASK 7

(a) **Reply to query**

> Dear Liam
>
> With regard to your business records, you are required to keep them for 5 years from the filing date for each return. For example, your records for 2014/15 should be kept until 31 January 2021 (i.e. 5 years from the normal filing date of 31 January 2016). I would therefore advise you to retain your business tax records as failure to so do can lead to a penalty of up to £3,000.
>
> Should you wish to delay your next balancing payment by 2 months, you will incur interest and penalties. Interest on the amount not paid will be payable from the due date until the date of payment. In addition, if you delay your balancing payment by more than 30 days you will also incur a penalty, as well as interest. The penalty is calculated as 5% of the amount of tax overdue.
>
> Please contact me again if you require further advice.

(b) **Dominic**

	True	False
The maximum penalty for mistakes in a tax return due to carelessness is 50%		✓
A company with a period of account ending 30 September 2016 must pay a penalty of up to £3,000 if it does not retain its records until 30 September 2021	✓	
Interest is charged on late payment of balancing payments only, not payments on account		✓
If an individual's balancing payment for 2015/16 is two months late they can be charged a late payment penalty of 5% of tax due	✓	
If an individual is eight months late in submitting their tax return for 2015/16, they will receive a penalty of £200		✓
Only AAT members not students are governed by the AAT ethical code		✓
There are no circumstances in which client confidentiality can be breached		✓

Tutorial note

The maximum penalty for incorrect returns depends on the behaviour of the taxpayer, and is calculated as a percentage of tax lost as follows:

(i)   Mistake – no penalty

(ii)   Failure to take reasonable care – 30%

(iii)   Deliberate understatement – 70%

(iv)   Deliberate understatement with concealment – 100%.

A company must retain their records for six years after the end of the chargeable accounting period. The maximum penalty for not retaining records is up to £3,000.

*Late payment interest is charged on **all** late payments of tax at a daily rate from the due date to the date of payment.*

It is the late payment penalty that is only levied on balancing payments (of income tax, class 2 and 4 NICs and capital gains tax) and not payments on account.

The amount due Is:

(i)   5% of the unpaid tax if it is more than one month late

(ii)   A further 5% if more than six months late

(iii)   A further 5% if more than 12 months late.

Penalties for submitting an individual's tax return late are as follows:

(i)   Within 3 months of the due date   =   £100 fixed penalty

(ii)   Between 3 to 6 months of the due date   =   Additional daily penalties of £10 per day
                                                                                (Maximum 90 days)

(iii)   Between 6 to 12 months of due date   =   Additional 5% of tax due (Minimum £300)

(iv)   More than 12 months after the due date   =   Additional 5% of tax due (Minimum £300)

(v)   More than 12 months after the due date if the taxpayer withholds information:

*   – deliberate and concealed = 100% (Minimum £300)*

*   – deliberate and not concealed = 70% (Minimum £300).*

The duty of confidentiality can be breached for legal or regulatory reasons (e.g. money laundering).

TASK 8

Tax calculation

Turnover

145 Total turnover from trade	£	920000 · 0 0
150 Banks, building societies, insurance companies and other financial concerns – *put an 'X' in this box if you do not have a recognised turnover and have not made an entry in box 145*		

Income

155 Trading profits	£	538200 · 0 0
160 Trading losses brought forward claimed against profits	£	72000 · 0 0
165 Net trading profits – *box 155 minus box 160*	£	466200 · 0 0
170 Bank, building society or other interest, and profits from non-trading loan relationships	£	18400 · 0 0
172 Put an 'X' in box 172 if the figure in box 170 is net of carrying back a deficit from a later accounting period		
175 Annual payments not otherwise charged to Corporation Tax and from which Income Tax has not been deducted	£	· 0 0

Income *continued*

180 Non-exempt dividends or distributions from non–UK resident companies	£	· 0 0
185 Income from which Income Tax has been deducted	£	· 0 0
190 Income from a property business	£	185000 · 0 0
195 Non-trading gains on intangible fixed assets	£	· 0 0
200 Tonnage Tax profits	£	· 0 0
205 Income not falling under any other heading	£	· 0 0

Chargeable gains

210 Gross chargeable gains	£	101000 · 0 0
215 Allowable losses including losses brought forward	£	· 0 0
220 Net chargeable gains – *box 210 minus box 215*	£	101000 · 0 0

Profits before deductions and reliefs

225 Losses brought forward against certain investment income	£	· 0 0
230 Non-trade deficits on loan relationships (including interest) and derivative contracts (financial instruments) brought forward	£	· 0 0
235 Profits before other deductions and reliefs – *net sum of boxes 165 to 205 and 220 minus sum of boxes 225 and 230*	£	770600 · 0 0

TASK 9

(a)   **Lena**

	Chargeable asset	Exempt asset
Antique sideboard – sold for £23,000 to an auction house	✓	
Vintage classic car – Morris Minor worth £55,000 – gifted to daughter		✓
Unquoted shares in Febroy Ltd – sold for less than they were bought for	✓	
Treasury stock quoted on the UK stock exchange – sold on the open market for considerably more than it was bought for		✓
Holiday home in Wales – sold at a profit to neighbours. Lena lives in her main residence in Birmingham	✓	

Tutorial note

The sideboard is a chattel (i.e. tangible moveable property), but it is not exempt from capital gains tax as it was not purchased and sold for less than £6,000.

Cars are exempt assets, whether sold or gifted is not relevant; there is no chargeable gain or allowable loss arising on the disposal.

Unquoted shares are chargeable assets, whether they are sold for a gain or loss is not relevant.

Treasury stock is exempt from capital gains tax, whether a capital profit or loss is made on the disposal is not relevant.

An individual's principal private residence is exempt from capital gains tax, but not a second, holiday home.

(b)   Answer = D

Working: Chargeable gain computation

	£
Sale proceeds	8,450
Less: Cost	(3,180)
	5,270
Less: Indexation allowance (£3,180 × 0.244)	(776)
Chargeable gain	4,494
Chargeable gain cannot exceed: 5/3 × (£8,450 – £6,000)	4,083

Tutorial note

Where a non-wasting chattel is sold for more than £6,000 and it cost less than £6,000; a normal chargeable gain computation is required.

However, the gain cannot exceed the 5/3rd rule as shown above.

(c) **Vincent – Chargeable gain computation**

	£
Sale proceeds	235,000
Less: Cost £168,000 × (£235,000/(£235,000 + £320,000))	(71,135)
Less: Indexation allowance (£71,135 × 0.541)	(38,484)
Chargeable gain	125,381

TASK 10

Chargeable gain computation

	£
Sale of 400 shares matched with purchase in previous 9 days	
Sale proceeds (400 × £16.80)	6,720
Cost (400 × £15.50)	(6,200)
Unindexed gain	520
Less: Indexation allowance (N/A for previous 9 day purchases)	0
Chargeable gain	520
Sale of 350 shares from the pool	
Sale proceeds (350 × £16.80)	5,880
Less: Cost (W)	(2,900)
Unindexed gain	2,980
Less: Indexation allowance (W) (£3,428 – £2,900)	(528)
Chargeable gain	2,452
Total gain (£520 + £2,452)	2,972

Working: Share pool

	Number of shares	Cost £	Indexed cost £
July 2010	1,500	14,500	14,500
May 2011			
Bonus issue (1 for 6)	250	Nil	Nil
	1,750	14,500	14,500
Indexed rise July 2010 to Nov 2016			
0.182 × £14,500			2,639
	1,750	14,500	17,139
November 2015			
Disposal	(350)		
(350/1,750) × £14,500/£17,139		(2,900)	(3,428)
Balance c/f	1,400	11,600	13,711

Tutorial note

The matching rules for a company specify that disposals of shares are matched with:

1   purchases on the same day, and then

2   purchases in the previous 9 days (LIFO basis), and then

3   shares held in the share pool.

No indexation is given for shares matched with purchases on the same day or previous 9 days.

Indexation allowance is not required before recording a bonus issue, but is required before recording the disposal.

TASK 11

(a)   Answer = A

Working:

Chargeable at time of disposal = Lower of

(i)   Chargeable gain = £370,000

(ii)   Sale proceeds not reinvested = (£950,000 – £900,000) = £50,000

i.e. £50,000

Rollover relief is therefore the remaining gain:

(£370,000 – £50,000) = £320,000

Tutorial note

A   Correct answer.

B   The time limit for reinvestment expires in October 2019; therefore a purchase in November 2019 is too late to qualify.

C   Qualifying assets for rollover relief purposes do not include shares.

D   A claim must be made for rollover relief; it is not automatic.

(b)   (i)   **Taxable gain**

	£
Chargeable gains (£23,000 + £14,500)	37,500
Less: Current year allowable losses (Note)	(2,600)
	34,900
Less: Capital losses brought forward	(5,600)
Net chargeable gain	29,300
Less: Annual exempt amount	(11,100)
Taxable gain	18,200

(ii)   **Capital loss left to carry forward**

Loss on disposal to brother (Note)	3,000

Tutorial note

The loss arising on the disposal to the brother is a connected person loss.

It cannot be set against other gains. It can only be carried forward and set against gains arising from disposals to the same brother in the future.

(c) (i) **Capital gains tax liability**

	£
Capital gains	26,000
Less: Annual exempt amount	(11,100)
Taxable gains	14,900

£	£ p
1,785 (W) × 10%	178.50
13,115 × 20%	2,623.00
14,900	2,801.50

Working

	£
Basic rate band	32,000
Less: Taxable income	(30,215)
Basic rate band unused	1,785

Tutorial note

Capital gains on assets other than residential property are taxed at 10% if they fall below the basic rate threshold and 20% if they fall above the threshold. The corresponding rates for residential property are 18% and 28%.

(ii) Due date of payment is 31 January 2018